First World War
and Army of Occupation
War Diary
France, Belgium and Germany

41 DIVISION
Divisional Troops
Divisional Signal Company
1 March 1918 - 27 September 1919

WO95/2627/2

The Naval & Military Press Ltd
www.nmarchive.com
Published in association with The National Archives

Published by

The Naval & Military Press Ltd

Unit 10 Ridgewood Industrial Park,

Uckfield, East Sussex,

TN22 5QE England

Tel: +44 (0) 1825 749494

www.naval-military-press.com

www.nmarchive.com

This diary has been reprinted in facsimile from the original. Any imperfections are inevitably reproduced and the quality may fall short of modern type and cartographic standards.

© Crown Copyright
Images reproduced by permission of The National Archives, London, England, 2015.

Contents

Document type	Place/Title	Date From	Date To
Heading	WO95/2627/2		
Heading	41 Division Divl. Signal Coy 1918 Mar-1919 Sept. Missing 1918 Oct To 1919 Mar From Italy		
Heading	41st Divisional Signal Company, R.E. March 1918		
War Diary	Camposampiero	01/03/1918	01/03/1918
War Diary	Train	02/03/1918	05/03/1918
War Diary	Couturelle	06/03/1918	07/03/1918
War Diary	Lucheux	08/03/1918	20/03/1918
War Diary	Baizieux	21/03/1918	21/03/1918
War Diary	Favreuil	22/03/1918	22/03/1918
War Diary	Grevillers	23/03/1918	23/03/1918
War Diary	Achiet Le-Petit	24/03/1918	24/03/1918
War Diary	Bucquoy	25/03/1918	25/03/1918
War Diary	Souastre	26/03/1918	26/03/1918
War Diary	Bienvillers	27/03/1918	27/03/1918
War Diary	Bailleulval	27/03/1918	27/03/1918
War Diary	St Amand	28/03/1918	31/03/1918
War Diary	Field	01/03/1918	26/03/1918
Miscellaneous	122 Inf Bdes. St Jefferies		
Heading	41st Divisional Signal Company R.E. April 1918		
War Diary	St Amand	01/04/1918	02/04/1918
War Diary	En Route For 2nd Army	03/04/1918	04/04/1918
War Diary	Steenwoorde	04/04/1918	09/04/1918
War Diary	Canal Bank Ypres	10/04/1918	14/04/1918
War Diary	Vlamertinghe Chateau	15/04/1918	26/04/1918
War Diary	10 Elms Camp	27/04/1918	30/04/1918
War Diary	Field	02/04/1918	30/04/1918
Miscellaneous	Appendices. A.B.C.D.		
Heading	41st. Divisional. Signal. Coy. Visual Wireless & Power Buzzer & Amplifier Communications.		
Diagram etc			
Diagram etc	41st Divisional Signal Coy. Communications.		
Diagram etc			
Miscellaneous	Overhearing Of Telephone And Telegraph Messages By The Enemy.	16/04/1918	16/04/1918
Miscellaneous	O.C. 41st Dis Sig. Bn	29/04/1918	29/04/1918
Diagram etc			
War Diary	Lovie Chateau	01/05/1918	31/05/1918
War Diary	Field	01/05/1918	31/05/1918
Map	Visual & Wireless Communications. Appendix B		
Map	Appendix. B.		
Map	Appendix H		
Miscellaneous	Appendix. H.		
Map	Appendix E		
Map			
Miscellaneous	Appendix. E.		
Miscellaneous	C.C. 41st Div Sig Co	12/05/1918	12/05/1918
Miscellaneous	Syllabus For P.B Amplifier Class		

Type	Description	Start	End
Miscellaneous	Scheme Showing Telephonic Communications Between 41st. Divisional O.Ps And Liaison With Left Division Field And Heavy Artillery	14/05/1918	14/05/1918
Miscellaneous	41st. Divisional Defence Scheme Communications.		
Miscellaneous	Wireless And Power Bugger Communications.		
War Diary	Lovie Chateau	01/06/1918	04/06/1918
War Diary	Nieurlet	05/06/1918	07/06/1918
War Diary	Eperlecques	08/06/1918	26/06/1918
War Diary	Oudezeele	27/06/1918	30/06/1918
War Diary		02/06/1918	26/06/1918
Operation(al) Order(s)	41st Signal Coy Order No 38	03/06/1918	03/06/1918
Miscellaneous	122nd Infantry Brigade. Appendix B	05/06/1918	05/06/1918
Operation(al) Order(s)	41 Divl Signal Coy Order No 39 Appendix C	07/06/1918	07/06/1918
Miscellaneous	123rd Infantry Brigade Scheme On 18th June 1918.	17/06/1918	17/06/1918
Miscellaneous	To O/C No 3 Scan. 41st Divl Signal Co R.E. H/Qs 123 Inf Bde (For Information). Appendix E	18/06/1918	18/06/1918
Operation(al) Order(s)	41st Divisional Signal Coy. Order No. X. 2. Appendix F.	19/06/1918	19/06/1918
Miscellaneous	Notes On Signal Communications 122nd Infantry Brigade Scheme Carried Out 20th June 1918.	20/06/1918	20/06/1918
Operation(al) Order(s)	41st Divl Signal Coy Order No 40 Appendix H	25/06/1918	25/06/1918
Miscellaneous	122nd Infantry Brigade Appendix J	28/06/1918	28/06/1918
Heading	On His Majesty's Service. War Diary 41. Div. 'A'		
Heading	41 D Signals Vol 27 July 18		
War Diary	Oudezeele	01/07/1918	01/07/1918
War Diary	Le Linge	02/07/1918	07/07/1918
War Diary	Hut Camp & K 24 83.2 Sheet. 27.1	08/07/1918	09/07/1918
War Diary	Hut Camp	09/07/1918	31/07/1918
War Diary	Le Linge	02/07/1918	31/07/1918
Diagram etc	Diagram Of Proposed Bury Shts. 28 NW. S.W. Scale 1/20000 Appendix B		
Diagram etc	Wireless Amplifier & Power Buzzer-Communications		
Diagram etc	Appendix D Visual Communications 41st Divisional Signal Coy.		
Diagram etc	Route Diagram 41st Divisional Signal Coy. Appendix E		
Miscellaneous	Appendix. E.		
Map	Appendix F		
Diagram etc	Wireless Power Buzzer & Amplifier Communications. Appendix H		
Diagram etc	Appendix G		
War Diary	Hut Camp K 24 C 2.3	01/08/1918	29/08/1918
War Diary	Wizernes	30/08/1918	31/08/1918
War Diary	Hut Camp K 24 C 2.3.	01/08/1918	30/08/1918
Miscellaneous	Proposed Communications For 122nd Infantry Brigade Operation Order No. 209.		
Diagram etc			
Miscellaneous	Scherpenberg-La Clytte Lateral Bury Arrangements.		
Miscellaneous	Officers Duty Roster		
Operation(al) Order(s)	41st Divl Signal Co R.E. Order No. 41	27/08/1918	27/08/1918
War Diary	Wizernes	01/09/1918	02/09/1918
War Diary	Douglas Camp L14.a.2.0	03/09/1918	27/09/1918
War Diary	Mersey Farm	28/09/1918	29/09/1918
War Diary	Lankhof Farm	29/09/1918	30/09/1918
War Diary		04/09/1918	30/09/1918
Operation(al) Order(s)	41st Divisional Signal Co. RE. Order No 42 Appendix A		

Diagram etc	P.5 & Amplifier Communications 41st. Division.		
Miscellaneous	Appendix. C.		
Miscellaneous	Instruction No. Signalling Arrangement In The 41st Divl Area	14/09/1918	14/09/1918
Miscellaneous	Signalling Arrangements In The 41st. Divl. Area. Artillery Communications.		
Miscellaneous	Signalling Arrangements In The 41st Divisional Area. Machine Gun Communications.		
Miscellaneous	Signal Instructions No 43 Appendix E		
Miscellaneous	Duty Of Officers. Appendix 'A'		
War Diary	Cologne	10/04/1919	27/09/1919

WD95/2/27/2

41 DIVISION

DIVL. SIGNAL COY

1918 MAR — 1919 SEPT

✗ MISSING 1918 OCT TO 1919 MAR

FROM ITALY

Box 2627

Company returned with
Div. from Italy 1/5.3.18.

WAR DIARY

41st DIVISIONAL SIGNAL COMPANY, R.E.

M A R C H

1 9 1 8

Army Form C. 2118.

WAR DIARY
or
INTELLIGENCE SUMMARY.

(Erase heading not required.)

Instructions regarding War Diaries and Intelligence Summaries are contained in F. S. Regs., Part II. and the Staff Manual respectively. Title pages will be prepared in manuscript.

Place	Date	Hour	Summary of Events and Information	Remarks and references to Appendices
CAMPOSAMPIERO	1/3/18		Entrained at 2pm. Train started for France 4.39pm	
TRAIN	2/3/18 3/3/18 4/3/18 5/3/18		Passed through MILAN, TURIN, MÔDANE, AIX LES BAINS, BOURG, CHALONS sur MARNE, ÉPERNAY, AMIENS, DOULLENS. Detrained at 9am at MONDICOURT. Marched to COUTURELLE arrived 12. noon	
COUTURELLE	6/3/18.		Division is in IVth Corps, 3rd Army area. Telephone 122 Bde arrived. 124 Bde arrived. Also to 124 Bde communication arranged into Corps through Army.	
	7/3/18		Nothing to report	
LUCHEUX	8/3/18		Moved to LUCHEUX. Moved off 9am arrived 10.45am. 123 Bde arrived	
	9/3/18		Major Aitchison returned from leave	
	10/3/18		Capt Patrick left on a months leave to England	
	11/3/18		A/t Jefferies arrived back from leave.	
	12/3/18		Nothing to report	
	13/3/18		Artillery arrived and established H/qrs at GEZAINCOURT. Visual opened to them from Divn at 11am. OC visited 25th Divnl Area.	
	14/3/18		Nothing to report	
	15/3/18		Nothing to report	
	16/3/18		OC inspected Company in full marching order	
	17/3/18		Nothing to report	
	18/3/18		Nothing to report	

Base Records

Ref. Sheets 57.C.D.
1/40000

Army Form C. 2118.

WAR DIARY
or
INTELLIGENCE SUMMARY.
(Erase heading not required.)

Instructions regarding War Diaries and Intelligence Summaries are contained in F. S. Regs., Part II. and the Staff Manual respectively. Title pages will be prepared in manuscript.

Place	Date	Hour	Summary of Events and Information	Remarks and references to Appendices
LUCHEUX	19/3/18 20/3/18		Orders were received late in the evening on the 20/3/18 and to concentrate the BAIZIEUX area just west of ALBERT. Horse transport to move by 1st night.	
BAIZIEUX	21/3/18		All horse transport marched at 1pm under G.[illeg] Liphook for the night at 10.30 p.m. Divl H.Q. arrived at BAIZIEUX during the day. The dismounted personnel of the Divn under Lt Jefferies moving by rail were transported to HOUZE le BOM via Corbie on 21st. Inst and on 22nd orders were received. Lieut moved to [illeg] of the parties of the IV Corps transport received I.Q. to divert to the relief left BAIZIEUX by road 6.30 a.m. with orders to move to BIHUCOURT Div H.Q. moved with Signal Section to FAVREUIL and there march into the Div H.Q. to be at in support of the 6 Div V. Infantry appear to have broken through the battle zone in front of the 6th Corps and to have advanced well further on the right Corps situation for a decision from a more contentious nature [illeg] and mounted personnel arrived at BIHUCOURT at 5pm and told either a longer march.	
FAVREUIL	22/3/18		The dismounted personnel in the interim had not yet arrived and the office at FAVREUIL was working owing to the 6th Div lines with [illeg] the dismounted personnel came by motor lorry from Germany and moved back to GREVILLERS. Divl H.Q. was sheltered at close range, and a house which was vacated by the IV Corps. We have 3 B.A.Gs now billeted in FAVREUIL. The only commands in [illeg] lines upon the windows which in a nothing week. Signal Off H.Q. + Nos. Sec. for the personnel still at BAIZIEUX concentrate at GREVILLERS just after midnight. at 3 am the open line working to Battn was shot down.	
GREVILLERS	23/3/18		but lines at once came through under heavy Shellfire between Battn H.Q. and Brigades	

WAR DIARY
or
INTELLIGENCE SUMMARY.
(Erase heading not required.)

Army Form C. 2118.

Place	Date	Hour	Summary of Events and Information	Remarks and references to Appendices
GREVILLERS	23/3/18		Bdes. were Right 85 East return lines and were Held through the 24 hours — Troops devoted to duty of the Rearguard. He at last seemed tired, were shelled. Stretchers were communication were never broken. To more than harrass after fom. There has been very heavy fighting all day, the Bde Hqs repulsing successive attacks. The line had been broken on our left, on our right the German have crossed Bapaume. About 5 pm this Bn. moved back to ACHIET LE PETIT and Bde HQ brought up to BIHUCOURT. During the new arrangements of the Brigade gained two cable in two lair Bridge 85 East returning, these across country by the wood south, being from BIHUCOURT to ACHIET LE PETIT.	
ACHIET LE PETIT	24/3/18		About 9 pm to 3 am it reached the lamp Spelling stations communication between Bde + O.P.s late at night Bde HQ took up in Bihucourt, and wireless communication was maintained with Bde. The Germans turning to movement on our right wire in Bihucourt and HQ took up in a trench south eastward of our line. At 6 am Bn. HQ moved back to BUCQUOY + Bdes were ordered to get back to Standard trench HR 22 b 23 Bn the LE PETIT in the former positions under the HR. Unfortunately — time took no did not get up to the place orders and communication was broken down — for most of the day. Lines between BUCQUOY + ACHIET LE PETIT were maintained during the Rearrain to Bury of the tramway, telephone wire communication to the new Bde also to Bde of the brigade brought it up in position to ACHIET LE PETIT at 10 am. He was not due lines as they were vacated by the troops were used by the other Battalions.	
BUCQUOY	25/3/18			

Army Form C. 2118.

WAR DIARY
or
INTELLIGENCE SUMMARY.
(Erase heading not required.)

Instructions regarding War Diaries and Intelligence Summaries are contained in F. S. Regs., Part II. and the Staff Manual respectively. Title pages will be prepared in manuscript.

Place	Date	Hour	Summary of Events and Information	Remarks and references to Appendices
BUCQUOY	25/3		During the operations 22/25 the notes of all ranks worked with untiring energy and gallantry. No case has come to light of Men failing to deliver a message.	
SOUASTRE	26/3		At 6am the H. Run was relieved in the trenches by 43 In. and temporary took up Quarters Bde HQ at FONQUEVILLERS. At 9am report was received that German cavalry (?) broken through & were already on the outskirts of SOUASTRE. It turned out the Signal Coy was down back to St AMAND, the personnel of the Signal Office passing co one effective man to work the lines & the runners out with Regts and another the Stations known to be at Bde. It was apparent to our men that the German Cavalry was a myth.	
BIENVILLERS	27/3	12 noon	12 noon Bde HQ moved to BIENVILLERS at 2.30 pm to BAILLEUVAL and cable communication on the Existing open lines was established to the Brigades Bde HQ. Our the 27th Suffs. Bde were Bivouacked [illegible] of BIENVILLERS. Communication by Wireless by the Forward	
BAILLEUVAL			Bde HQ.NR in BIENVILLERS. Communication by Wireless by the Forward Exchange his. Orders were received at 6.30 am to etc. to be ready to	
St AMAND	28/3		At 8 on into ale lodging [illegible] Live feet east of BUCQUOY from AM orders Lou, am alt HQ moved to St AMAND Brigades in GOMMECOUR at the Siddany holding a line of trenches behind Ls Sefeech and cable comm laid from HQ at 6 pm as far as possible off the road from BIENVILLERS to GROYES Bde HQ. Post Station and Lomanne Bee was situated in BIENVILLERS and St AMAND connected BIENVILLERS to St AMAND by the link cable only. One across country. In this manner news communication into existence & from	
	29/3		post at 6 pm. Wireless communication was also through. 29th A. Quiet day all Comm. all pm then Running Laboratory. In the Afternoon H/Q have were comm at St AMAND connected 30th Moving Messengers 42 Bees in the line towards to relieve	

WAR DIARY
or
INTELLIGENCE SUMMARY
(Erase heading not required.)

Army Form C. 2118.

Place	Date	Hour	Summary of Events and Information	Remarks and references to Appendices
ST AMAND	29/7/14		Arrangements were made to give 19th Inf Bde at St AMAND its communication with Corps H.Q. at ST OMER. Other lines were laid to a forward signal office at HENNESCAMP, to minimise the danger of losing our lines to Brigades. A cable loop was laid from the HENNESCAMP office to the Post Station at BIENVILLERS. This line was kept on the Artillery wagons at BIENVILLERS. When the enemy line was cut near the tramway at BIENVILLERS put the line through on the cable loop until the Regiment could be again restored. Great efforts were made to use somewhere the two lines owing to the good telephone communication afforded. Between HENNESCAMP & BIENVILLERS, the two lines handed over by F.A. 44 were commenced to be difficult to maintain, but 23 Officers who were to go to tramways ran along them and were consequently cut 29 Officers rejoining well away from the road. Station was ordered to lay a 2nd line to BIENVILLERS Keeping well away from the road avoiding battery positions. The line was only cut on a occasions & was excellent between Essent & DHQ and that remains though someway roundabout. In a of the Laum shelling. It was very remarkable how unreached was our line in Amiens area escaped. Toward of 6th Div HQ The Bow Bryzen and Brentham Rest in Amiens by the 70 Div were exceedingly well and normal communication was established between Bdes Battalion in both Bdes. The line that the been broken. Overhead were commencing laid above to whether letters Bdes- Battalion and the line cut through. Immediately the wagon of morths the Horse Line quite a little communication will care looking as in Battalion and line was the telephone conversation All messages of interest coming were copied- from telephone at HENNESCAMP, hence to Bde & Bdes Orders & Bde to Bde of the 19 of Sept	
	30/7/14		...	

Army Form C. 2118.

WAR DIARY
or
INTELLIGENCE SUMMARY.
(Erase heading not required.)

Instructions regarding War Diaries and Intelligence Summaries are contained in F. S. Regs., Part II. and the Staff Manual respectively. Title pages will be prepared in manuscript.

Place	Date	Hour	Summary of Events and Information	Remarks and references to Appendices
Field	1. 3/5		1 O.R. to Hosp. Sick	
"	24 3/5		2 OR Butcher killed in action	
"	24 3/5		3 OR missing	
"			1 OR wounded + evacuated	
"	29/5		1 OR to Hosp. Ot Sick	
"	26/5		2 L.C. Volitals joined from L.C. Bn.	

Secret

HS 333

Sigs 122 Inf Bdes.   Lt Jeffreys
      123   "   "   Lt Stanworth
      124   "   "   Lt Sylvester
  "   42 DIVN   CSM.

(I) 41 DIV will relieve 42 Div in the line on night 29/30 March.

(II) A forward divisional signals station will be established at HANNESCAMPS. There will be a telegraph office at above place and all telegrams will be sent by runner to & from this office.
Lt Jeffreys will be in charge of the forward signal station & will have with him the following
1 N.C.O. 4 linemen. 2 motor cyclists
3 OTs. 2 mounted orderlies
2 push cyclists.

(III) 1 NCO & 2 linemen will be established at new hqrs of 124 bde for maintenance of lateral line to GOMMECOURT as far as PIGEON WOOD E23D0·2, and the lines to HANNESCAMPS in conjunction with the linesmen from the forward signal station.

(IV) A wireless station working to the

(IV) DIVN will be established near new 124 Bde Hqrs.

(V) The personnel now at BIENVILLERS station (less one linesman) will withdraw to DHQ when 41 Divn takes over the line.
One lineman will be left to assist Signals 42 Divn until 12 noon 30/3/18

(VI) The wireless station now at GOMMECOURT will be withdrawn to DHQ on relief by a wireless set of 42 DIVN.

(VII) One DR lineman now at GOMMECOURT will remain with 42 DIV until 12 noon 30.3.18.

(VIII) Brigade lines will be taken over under mutual arrangements between Brigade section Officers.
All amplifiers and power buzzers at present in action will be left in position by Signals 42 DIVN. Amplifier personnel will be sent to Sigs 123 & 124 Inf Bdes.

(IX) St Jeffries will be ready to take over the HANNESCAMP station at 12 midnight 29/30, and linemen will be in position at new 124 Bde Hqrs E24 D 8.8. at same hour.

(X) Each Brigade will send two runners to forward signal station at Hannescamps, directly the Brigades of 42 DIVN are relieved.

JWMcKay Major
OC Signals
41 Divn

41st Divisional Engineers

WAR DIARY

41st DIVISIONAL SIGNAL COMPANY R. E.

APRIL 1918

41st Divisional Engineers

41 D Signals
Vol 24

WAR DIARY
INTELLIGENCE SUMMARY
(Erase heading not required.)

Place	Date	Hour	Summary of Events and Information	Remarks and references to Appendices
S<u>T</u> AMAND	1/4/18		Lines are all working well.	
		3 p.m.	Enemy put down heavy barrage on the vicinity of HANNESCAMPS, which cut the then lines back to BIENVILLERS, but communications on the cable loop were not cut. Forward of HANNESCAMPS the three ground lines to the four grouped Brigades in ESSARTS were cut. A lineman from the Divisional Forward Communication Post quickly mended the lines, and telephone communication was interrupted only for a space of 20 minutes. Wireless remained unbroken throughout the day. Arrangements were made for the crossover of the Divisional Section to pass to the G.O.C. of the 42<u>nd</u> Division at an early hour on the 2<u>nd</u> of April.	
	2/4/18	2 a.m.	Command of the Section passed and communications handed over to O.C. Signals 42<u>nd</u> Div<u>n</u>, all lines being through. All Power Buzzers & Amplifiers were left in position & handed over working to the relieving Brigades of the 42<u>nd</u> Div<u>n</u>. The Wireless Stations were taken out & replaced.	

WAR DIARY

INTELLIGENCE SUMMARY.

(Erase heading not required.)

Army Form C. 2118.

Place	Date	Hour	Summary of Events and Information	Remarks and references to Appendices
En route for 2nd Army	3/8		The Company entrained at PETIT HOUVIN at 9 p.m.	
	4/8		The Signals detrained at PESELHOEK at 9 a.m. and marched to STEENWOORDE. Excellent arrangements were found to have been made for us by AD Signals VIII Corps. Corps operators were in position, and lines were through to VIII Corps H/Q, via STEENWOORDE local exchange, and also to the positions allotted for Brigade H/Qs. Brigade Signals on arrival had only to pick up the lines, which were led into their Offices, when communication with the Division was established. This was an excellent example of how a good Corps Signals can help a Division moving quickly into a new area.	
STEENWOORDE	4/8		O.C. Div Signals reconnoitred forward areas in the YPRES salient with a view to taking over from the 29th Div at an early date.	

Army Form C. 2118.

WAR DIARY
INTELLIGENCE SUMMARY.
(Erase heading not required.)

Place	Date	Hour	Summary of Events and Information	Remarks and references to Appendices
STEENWOORDE	6/7/18	12 noon	The Signal Coy paraded at ECKE at 12 noon + were inspected by the VIII Corps Commander who complimented them on the smartness of their turn out + on the work done in the opening stages of the SOMME battle.	
	7/7/18		Further reconnaissances were carried out by officers of the Divisional Signal Coy in the 29th Div'n area.	
	8/7/18		Nothing special to report.	
	9/7/18		German attack on the 1st Army started. We relieved the 29th Div'n H/Bs Canal Bank at 12 midnight 9th/10th. The relief of necessity being a hurried one, owing to the departure of the 29th Div'n to reinforce the 1st Army which was heavily engaged.	

Army Form C. 2118.

WAR DIARY
INTELLIGENCE SUMMARY.
(Erase heading not required.)

Place	Date	Hour	Summary of Events and Information	Remarks and references to Appendices
Canal Bank YPRES	10/4/18		Communications in the area taken over from the 29th Divn are working satisfactorily & only minor alterations were found necessary	
	11/4/18		The Bn¹ HQ was shelled from 10:30 a.m. to 1:30 p.m. by 9.45" guns. The Signal NCOs mess was destroyed but fortunately there was nobody at home at the time. The situation on our right was uncomfortable	
	12/4/18 & 13/4/18		Nothing special to report. Buried lines working forward to Brigades are doing well. The Wireless is working from D.H.Q. to the two Brigades in the front line & to the Reserve Brigade at WIELTJE. Preparations are being made for communications in case of a withdrawal from PASSCHENDAELE RIDGE, which may be necessary owing to the situation further South	
	14/4/18		During the early hours our main line resistance was withdrawn in conjunction with the Divisions on our Rt & Lt to the front line of the main battle position.	

Army Form C. 2118.

WAR DIARY
INTELLIGENCE SUMMARY.
(Erase heading not required.)

Place	Date	Hour	Summary of Events and Information	Remarks and references to Appendices
Canal Bank YPRES	14/4/18		Outposts are being left in the old front line. Genl Clemson is in command of the outposts with HQ at GALLIPOLI and Genl Seagrith is in command of the troops manning the battle zone with his HQ at WIELTJE. Communication is through everywhere in the Division by the buried cable and also by wireless.	
VLAMERTINGHE Chateau	15/4/18		We withdrew at dusk to a line just in front of YPRES from the WHITE CHATEAU on the main road to WIELTJE. Divl HQ moved back to VLAMERTINGHE CHATEAU. The two front line Bdes have their HQ in the YPRES ramparts and 122 Bde in Reserve has its HQ near GOLDFISH CHATEAU. Buried lines are through and working to all Bttns & Bdes. Wireless is working from the ramparts at YPRES to Divl HQ and a third wireless station is in position and working at 10 ELMS CAMP, which will be the future position of Divl HQ should a further withdrawal become necessary. There are no buried cables further back than Divl HQ & two cross country lines were laid by cable wagons between VLAMERTINGHE CHATEAU and 10 ELMS CAMP.	

Army Form C. 2118.

WAR DIARY
or
INTELLIGENCE SUMMARY.
(Erase heading not required.)

Place	Date	Hour	Summary of Events and Information	Remarks and references to Appendices
VLAMERTINGHE CHATEAU	15/8		as a precaution in case further withdrawals were decided on. Prior to the withdrawal arrangements were made to demolish as far as possible the buried cables in advance of the OUTPOST LINE. By arrangements made with the C.R.E. the main test boxes and dugouts were blown up, & the lesser test boxes were destroyed by Mills grenades. Plants and fire, the route markers were removed and placed in a position well away from the actual buried cables. The Staff were worried that owing to the probability of the enemy having exhibitions fixed on to buried cables now in his possession that there sent great danger of his overhearing our telephone conversations anywhere near our line at D.H.Q. The Staff have sent out instructions cautioning all units on the danger of using the telephone, and any messages of at all a confidential nature are being sent either by D.R. or by fullerphones which are working to all Brigades	20/11/14 ATT95 B.C.

Army Form C. 2118.

WAR DIARY
INTELLIGENCE SUMMARY.
(Erase heading not required.)

Instructions regarding War Diaries and Intelligence Summaries are contained in F. S. Regs., Part II. and the Staff Manual respectively. Title pages will be prepared in manuscript.

Place	Date	Hour	Summary of Events and Information	Remarks and references to Appendices
VLAMERTINGHE CHATEAU	16/8		Lines from Div¹ H/Q forward were completed in accordance with Diagram Appendix A & B attached.	
			Very heavy Gas shelling in YPRES on the night 16/17 causing considerable casualties amongst Signal Personnel, especially amongst Linesmen working over ground which had been shelled by Mustard Gas. Indents were sent in for Rubber gloves to protect Linesmen's hands.	
	17/8		All communications working satisfactorily	
	18·19/ 8			
	/8		Nothing to report	
	20/8		YPRES again heavily shelled by Gas Shells during the night. Fifteen casualties chiefly amongst Wireless Personnel who had the Gas blankets at the entrance to their dug-out in the ramparts blown in by a Gas Shell	
	21/8		Gen¹ Williams U.S.A. Army staying with Div¹ H/Q, and System of Communications	

A6945 Wt. W11422/M1160 350,000 12/16 D. D. & L. Forms/C./2118/14

WAR DIARY
INTELLIGENCE SUMMARY.
(Erase heading not required.)

Army Form C. 2118.

Place	Date	Hour	Summary of Events and Information	Remarks and references to Appendices
VLAMERTINGHE CHATEAU	21/8			
	22/23		shown and explained to him by O/C Signals.	
			Nothing to report	
	24/8		A Signal school for Infantry beginners consisting of 5 officers + 40 ORs is being started at 10 ELMS CAMP.	
	25/8	2	Enemy opened hurricane bombardment at 2.30 a.m. extending from South of KEMMEL HILL to as far North as our Rt Brigade Sub-Sector.	
			KEMMEL was entered by the Germans from the French at 7 a.m. and a wireless message was received about 10 a.m. stating that the enemy were advancing on DICKEBUSH. This is untrue and seems to be German propaganda.	
			A good reconnaissance was carried out by Motor Cyclist Corporal Heslor in the area as far South as two Divisions on our right from whom no reports had been received. Situation was accurately reported by him.	

WAR DIARY
or
INTELLIGENCE SUMMARY.
(Erase heading not required.)

Army Form C. 2118.

Place	Date	Hour	Summary of Events and Information	Remarks and references to Appendices
VLAMERTINGHE CHATEAU	26/4/18		German capture of VOORMEZEELE necessitated the withdrawal of our outpost line at	
		6.30 p.m.	Divl H.Q. moved back to 10 ELMS, 124 Bde to ROME FARM, 122 + 123 Bdes to VLAMERTINGHE CHATEAU. Liaisons from 10 ELMS forward had already been prepared for this move, which offered no difficulties. Wireless was established as follows. Wilson directing set at 10 ELMS CAMP, with Trench Sets at VLAMERTINGHE CHATEAU and ROME FARM. Wireless communication was through at 8 a.m.	change
10 ELMS CAMP	27/4/18		Communication forward from 10 ELMS was enlarged + improved.	Swirl
	28/4/18		Nothing to report	
	29/4/18		Heavy enemy bombardment started at 3 a.m. all down the line, and at dawn the Germans attacked from MONT ROUGE to South of YPRES. An alarmist message from a liaison officer of the French Army, stating that the enemy had captured SCHERPENBERG, MONT ROUGE and MONT NOIR caused preparations	

Army Form C. 2118.

WAR DIARY
INTELLIGENCE SUMMARY.
(Erase heading not required.)

Place	Date	Hour	Summary of Events and Information	Remarks and references to Appendices
ELMS CAMP	30/4/18		to be made for an immediate occupation of the Blue line West of YPRES and Div' H.Q. moved back to LOVIE CHATEAU at 9 p.m. During the evening re-assuring reports were received from the French and from the British Divisions on our right and orders for the withdrawal to the West of YPRES were cancelled. Extra lines by Grand Cable between Div'n & Brigades were put through, care being taken to avoid shelled areas. Wireless communication is working between Div' H.Q and Brigades. The enemy has been very quiet all day and all communications are working in a very satisfactory manner.	

Armstrong Major
O.C. 41st Div'l Signal Co. R.E.

Army Form C. 2118.

WAR DIARY
or
INTELLIGENCE SUMMARY
(Erase heading not required.)

Place	Date	Hour	Summary of Events and Information	Remarks and references to Appendices
Field	2/8		1 OR Transferred to Signal Service T.C. Bedford	
	5/8		2 ORs reported missing on 24/3 rejoined Unit. 1 OR Transferred to Signal Service T.C. Bedford	
	9/8		1 OR Evacuated to C.C.S	
	9/8		2 ORs do	
	21/8		6 ORs from Base Signal Depot as reinforcements	
	13/8		1 OR admitted to Hosp.	
			2 ORs Evacuated to C.C.S	
	15/8		4 ORs do	
	18/8		4 " do	
	20/8		8 " do	
	21/8		2 " do + 1 OR Transferred to Signal Service T.C. Bedford	
	22/8		3 " do — 2 OR do	
	24/8		4 " from Base Signal Depot as reinforcements	
	21/8		1 OR Tpd to Signal Service T.C. Bedford	
	23/8		1 OR Awarded Military Medal	
	27/8		2 ORs Arrived from Base Signal Depot as reinforcements	
	28/8		6 ORs do	
	30/8		do	

Amour, O/C enfield Signal Co. R.E.

Appendices. A. B. C & D.

Appendix. B.

41ST DIVISIONAL SIGNAL COY.

VISUAL, WIRELESS,
& POWER BUZZER
& AMPLIFIER
COMMUNICATIONS.

DIV. HQ.
VLAMERTINGHE CHATEAU

W.

to 10 Elms Camp.

Appendix. A.

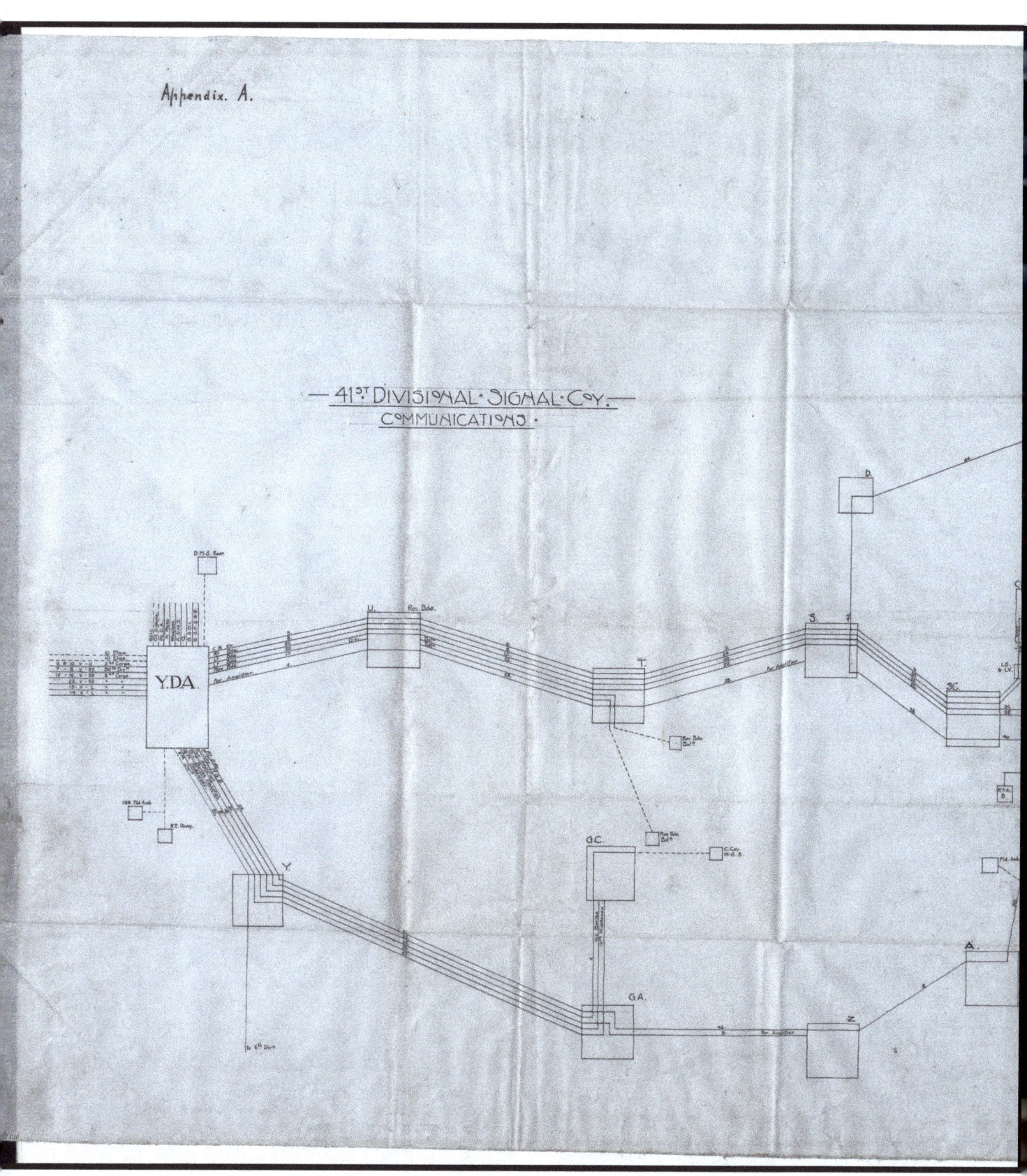

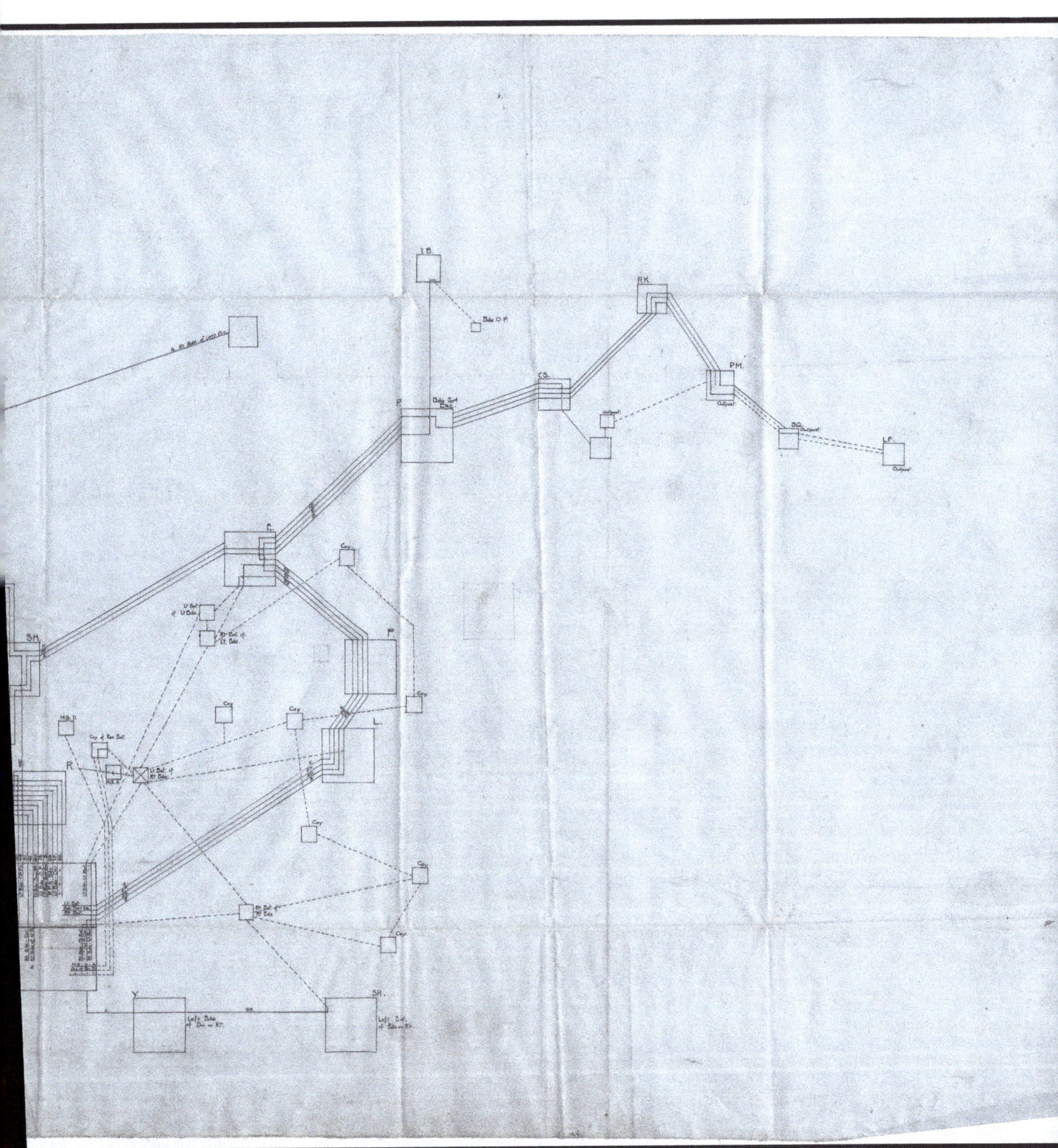

S E C R E T.
****

41st Div.
G. 149.
(34/2).

Subject: Overhearing of telephone and telegraph messages by the enemy.

1. Now that our troops have been withdrawn, there will be a great danger of telephone conversations being overheard by the enemy who will be occupying an area covered by an extensive system of our buried cables. Even the Fullerphone cannot be regarded as being safe East of YPRES and for telephone work anything East of VLAMERTINGHE must be regarded as dangerous.

2. Though every effort was made to destroy test points, the buried cables still remain and an amplifier fixed on to the end of any of them may enable anything to be overheard East of VLAMERTINGHE, which is the Western limit of the buried routes.

3. Unless the risk of being overheard by the enemy is of less importance than getting a message through at all costs, nothing is to be said on the telephone East of VLAMERTINGHE or sent by telegraph East of YPRES, that would give him information of any value.

16th April, 1918.

EaBeck.
Lieut.Colonel,
General Staff.

WM 99.   April 29ᵗʰ -18

O.C.
41ˢᵗ Div Sig Co

APPENDIX D

Sir,
    Herewith position & calls of the Wireless Power Buzzer and Amplifier Stations in this sector.

           W Stanworth Lieut
              R. Wireless
              41 Div Sig Co

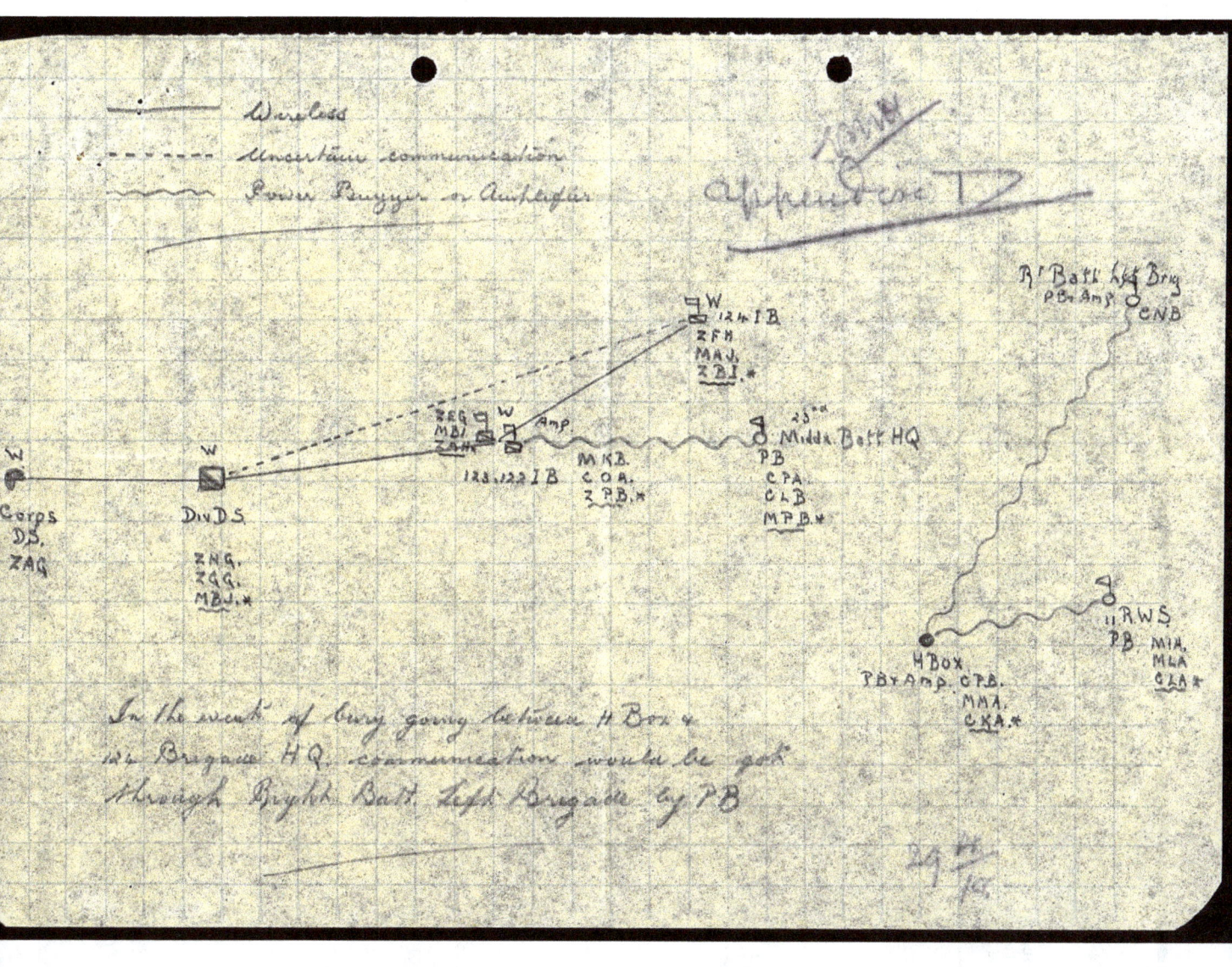

Appendix D

In the event of bury going between H Box & 124 Brigade HQ communication would be got through Right Batt. Left Brigade by PB

Army Form C. 2118.

Signals / D

Vol 24

WAR DIARY
or
INTELLIGENCE SUMMARY.
(Erase heading not required.)

Instructions regarding War Diaries and Intelligence Summaries are contained in F. S. Regs., Part II. and the Staff Manual respectively. Title pages will be prepared in manuscript.

Place	Date	Hour	Summary of Events and Information	Remarks and references to Appendices
LOUIE CHATEAU	1/5/18		A quiet day. Forward lines completed on 2nd Divn front to join the signs Appendix A not Appendix A	
	2/5/18		Wireless Power Buzzer and Visual Chain of forward communications completed as in Appendix B attached	Appendix B.
	3/5/18		O/C Signals visited Signal School at the Div'l Wing at MILLAIN. Very good progress is being made. Training is being carried out on lines of programme at once. Appendix C. 31st	Appendix C.
	4/5/18		Communications working satisfactorily. 1 Bar to Military Medal and 8 Military Medals awarded this day to the Signal Co.	
	5/5/18		124 Bde moved hqrs from VLAMERTINGHE CHATEAU to FOSTER CAMP N1662 at 6 p.m. Lines were adjusted as required by the new situation.	
	6/5/18		In order to provide safe communication in case of a withdrawal to Green Line, one Armoured Quad and 1 Twin Cable were laid from the cable head	

Army Form C. 2118.

WAR DIARY
INTELLIGENCE SUMMARY.
(Erase heading not required.)

Place	Date	Hour	Summary of Events and Information	Remarks and references to Appendices
LOVIE CHATEAU	6/5/18		about A26 Central to A27a 65.00 Thence NW in the Canal to A22c8.9 Thence SE in the route ROOBART BEEK to G5a 0.9 thence overground in ditches to the proposed Brigade H/Q for the Green Line in G6a. Visual was tested through between G5b 8.7 and A26 central.	
	7/5/18		Rather heavy shelling about 9 hrs brought down 3 forward routes between Div and Bdes. Communications were fully re-established about 6.30 am on 8th inst.	
	8/5/18		Heavy shelling of the Brit Area about 11 am of the line of the Batteries from down to 11am. This is in conjunction with the German attack on the junction of 22 Corps and French Army. The main Div! buried route via MACHINE GUN FARM was cut in front of ROME FARM at 9.8am. Communication on this bury was re-established during the afternoon.	
	9/5/18		Batt⁹ in the line were visited by O.C. Signals during the morning. All their communications	

WAR DIARY

or

INTELLIGENCE SUMMARY.

(Erase heading not required.)

Army Form C. 2118.

Place	Date	Hour	Summary of Events and Information	Remarks and references to Appendices
LOVIE CHATEAU	9/5/18		were working satisfactorily. Situation on the Divisional front quiet.	
	10/5/18		Nothing special to report.	
	11/5/18		122 Infy Bde sidestepped to the Right and handed over its original left Batn sector to 36th Div. The 124 Infy Bde came into the line on the Rt of the 122 Infy Bde, taking over from a Bde of the 6th Divn. Positions of Bde HQs are now as follows. 122 & 124 Infy Bdes at MACHINE GUN FARM. 123 Infy Bde in Reserve at VLAMERTINGHE CHATEAU. Communications were established in accordance with Appendices D & E attached, shewing wire, wireless, and visual communications.	Appendix D do E
	12/5/18		A Power Buzzer class of 20 OR from the Infy started at DHQ under the Divisional Wireless Officer. It is intended to select eight of the best men from this class to replace casualties in the Divisional Amplifier Section. The remaining men will rejoin the Infantry on	

WAR DIARY
INTELLIGENCE SUMMARY

(Erase heading not required.)

Army Form C. 2118.

Place	Date	Hour	Summary of Events and Information	Remarks and references to Appendices
LOVIE CHATEAU	12/5/18		Completion of course as Power Buzzer men. The syllabus of the course is attached vide Appendix 7	Appendix 7
			Heavy shelling of the Dirt Area about MACHINE GUN FARM cut the buried cables running forward from that point. This buey was put down in 1916, and though every effort was made to trace it, it could not be found.	
	13/5/18		It was found still impossible to find the route of the buey which was cut on the 12th inst., though the area detachment was reinforced by Drivers and every man available from A/B. No 1 Sections, and overground cables were run from a point where the buey was picked up at about H6 c.1.5 to the M.G. hqr at H5 c.b.7. By this means the tele forward communications were temporarily reestablished.	
	14/5/18		Div¹ O.P. Lines were completed in accordance with Diagram Appendix 9 attached	Appendix 9 attached
	15/5/18		A working party of 200 men was obtained from the 123 Inf.Bde and the overground cables forward of MACHINE GUN FARM were buried to an average depth of 4'.6" at which point water was struck.	

WAR DIARY
INTELLIGENCE SUMMARY.
(Erase heading not required.)

Army Form C. 2118.

Place	Date	Hour	Summary of Events and Information	Remarks and references to Appendices
LOVIE CHATEAU	15/5/18		Another working party will be obtained as soon as possible to break up this bivy so that it will be covered by 6ft of earth. All work in this area has to be done at night.	
	16/5/18		All communications are now working in a satisfactory manner. The Div'l Signal School moved from MILLAIN to RUBROUCK.	
	17/5/18		Wireless Communication was this day re-arranged so as to give a complete wireless chain from Div.H.Q. to front line. See Diagram. Appendix H attached.	Appendix H
	18/5/18		Nothing special to report	
	19/5/18		Two groups of War flags were sent to the Div'l Signal Co. One group is attached to each of the two Infantry Brigades in the line. A working party of 200 men worked and made tolerably safe the new buried cable route in the vicinity of MACHINE GUN FARM	

Army Form C. 2118.

WAR DIARY
INTELLIGENCE SUMMARY.

(Erase heading not required.)

Place	Date	Hour	Summary of Events and Information	Remarks and references to Appendices
LOVIE CHATEAU	20/5/18		Nothing to report	
	21/5/18		2 Lt Love joined the Coy and was posted to 190 R.F.A. Bde Sub Sec in place of Lt Morris returned to II Army	
			Heavy shelling of back areas caused several faults on the air lines which were quickly repaired	
	22 + 23/5/18		Nothing to report beyond the usual maintenance work caused by back area shelling	
	24/5/18		OC Signals went round all Batt.ns and Conferences in the line. Their communications are satisfactory	
	25/5/18		102 Infy Bde relieved the 124 Bde in the line at 5.30 p.m. All lines through and working satisfactorily	
	26/5/18		Nothing to report except heavy back area shelling which caused breaks on the air lines which were quickly repaired	

Army Form C. 2118.

WAR DIARY
or
INTELLIGENCE SUMMARY.
(Erase heading not required.)

Place	Date	Hour	Summary of Events and Information	Remarks and references to Appendices
LOVIE CHATEAU	27/5/18		Enemy attacked RIDGE WOOD and SCOTTISH WOOD at 3.30 a.m. and barrage. Our forward areas. Buried cable routes held throughout.	
	28/5/18		Arrangements have been made to send 3 Officers and 18 ORs from the Div'l Signal School to the Corps Signal School, and to start another class for 30 beginners at the Div'l Signal School.	
	29/5/18		Signal preparations are being made for the move of the two Artillery Bdes. from SALVATION CORNER and REIGERSBERG to MACHINE GUN FARM at H5a 0.5/8.5 respectively. The latter point is being joined to MG Coy near MACHINE GUN FARM by a buried cable route, the necessary working parties being found by the Gunners working under supervision of O/C Signals	
	30/5/18		Nothing to report	
	31/5/18		Orders were received at 6 p.m. for the relief of the 41st Div'n by XV Corps Artillery by the	

WAR DIARY or INTELLIGENCE SUMMARY

Army Form C. 2118.

Place	Date	Hour	Summary of Events and Information	Remarks and references to Appendices
LONE CHATEAU	31/5/18		49th Divn. Preliminary arrangements for handing over were made. A defence scheme is existent vide Appendix J attached	Appendix J

Army Form C. 2118.

WAR DIARY
or
INTELLIGENCE SUMMARY.
(Erase heading not required.)

Instructions regarding War Diaries and Intelligence Summaries are contained in F. S. Regs., Part II. and the Staff Manual respectively. Title pages will be prepared in manuscript.

Place	Date	Hour	Summary of Events and Information	Remarks and references to Appendices
Field	1/43			
	3/5/18		1 OR Arrived from Base Signal Depot	
	5/5/18		5 ORs transferred to S.S.T.C. Bedford	
	2/5/18		1 ORs Evacuated to C.C.S.	
	5/5/18		1 " " "	
	6/5/18		3 " Transferred to S.S.T.C. Bedford	
	6/5/18		6 " Arrived from Base Signal Depot. 1 Bar + 5 M.M.s awarded to Company	
	8/5/18		3 " Evacuated to C.C.S.	
			do. 1 Offr + 5 ORs arrived from Base Signal Depot. 1 OR evacuated to C.C.S.	
	7 "		4 " Arrived from Base Signal Depot. 1 OR evacuated to C.C.S	
	11 "		1 OR. Transferred from 26 DR to G.R.E. Signal Service	
	9/5/18		5. M.Ms awarded to Company.	
	12/5/18		4 ORs arrived from Base Signal Depot. 1 OR evacuated to C.C.S	
	14/5/18		6 " " " do	
	17 5/18		2 " " " do	
			18 ors. Transferred to R.E's in No. 6 Secn	
	18 5/18		" " " to S.S.T.C. Bedford 3 or evacuated to C.C.S	
	20 "		1 or. Arrived from 41st Div. M.T. Col.	
	21 5/18		4 ORs " " Base Signal Depot	
	2 "		1 Offr " " do. 1 Offr. repd to IV Army	
	24		1 OR " " do. 4 ors Offrs to S.S.T.C. Bedford	

(A8001) D. D. & L., London, E.C. Wt. W1771/M2031 750,000 5/17 Sch. 52 Forms/C2118/14

Army Form C. 2118.

WAR DIARY
INTELLIGENCE SUMMARY.
(Erase heading not required.)

Instructions regarding War Diaries and Intelligence Summaries are contained in F. S. Regs., Part II. and the Staff Manual respectively. Title pages will be prepared in manuscript.

Place	Date	Hour	Summary of Events and Information	Remarks and references to Appendices
Field	27/5/18		2 ORs arrive from Base Signal Dept.	
	29/5/18		1 do. do.	
	31/5/18		3 do. do.	

Armstrong Major
O.C. Signals
H.1 Division

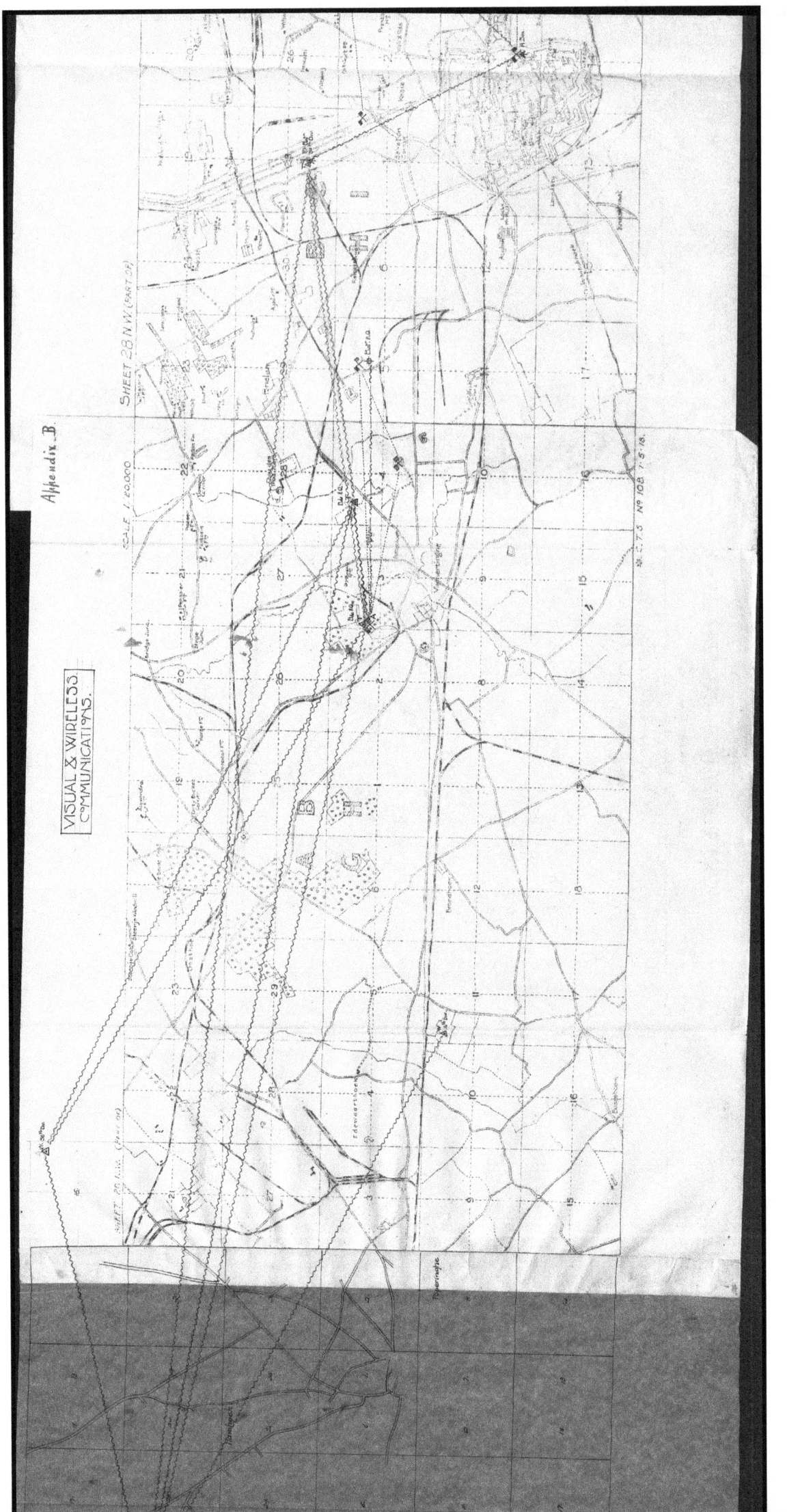

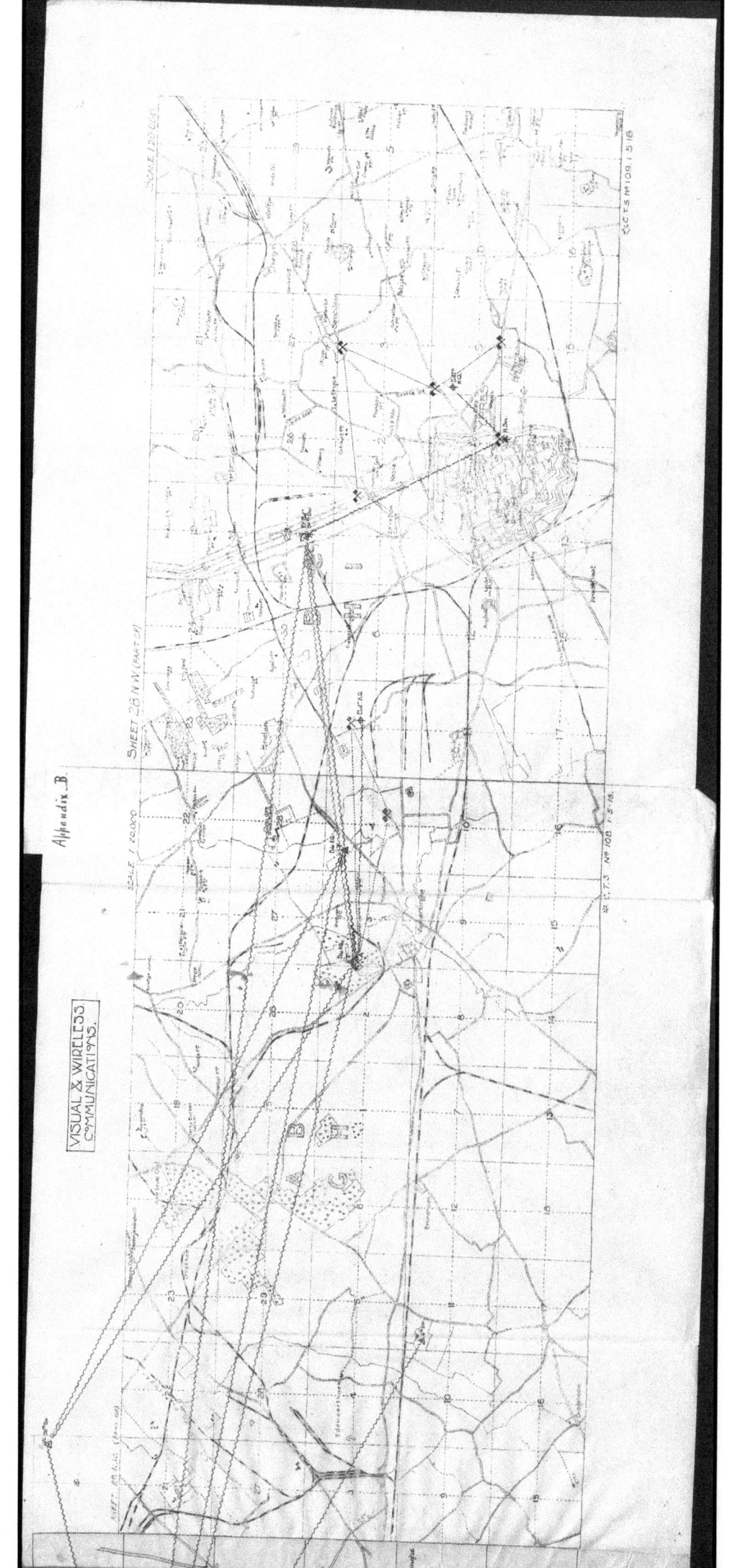

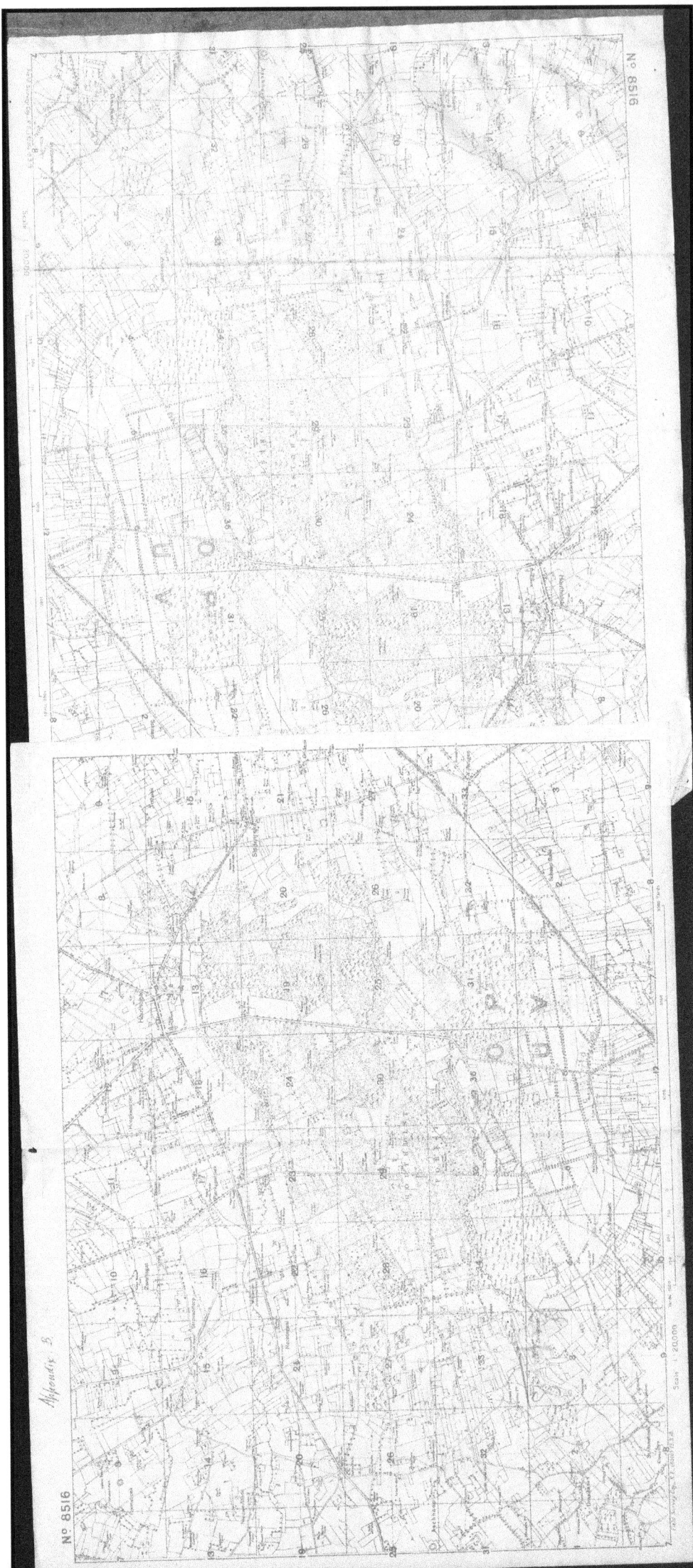

Appendix . H.

WIRELESS & POWER BUZZER
& AMPLIFIER COMMUNICATIONS.
18-5-18.

SCALE 1/20,000.

Appendix. A.

Appendix. A.

WIRELESS & POWER BUZZER
AMPLIFIER COMMUNICATIONS.
18-5-18.

SCALE 1:20000

Appendix. H.

Appendix E.

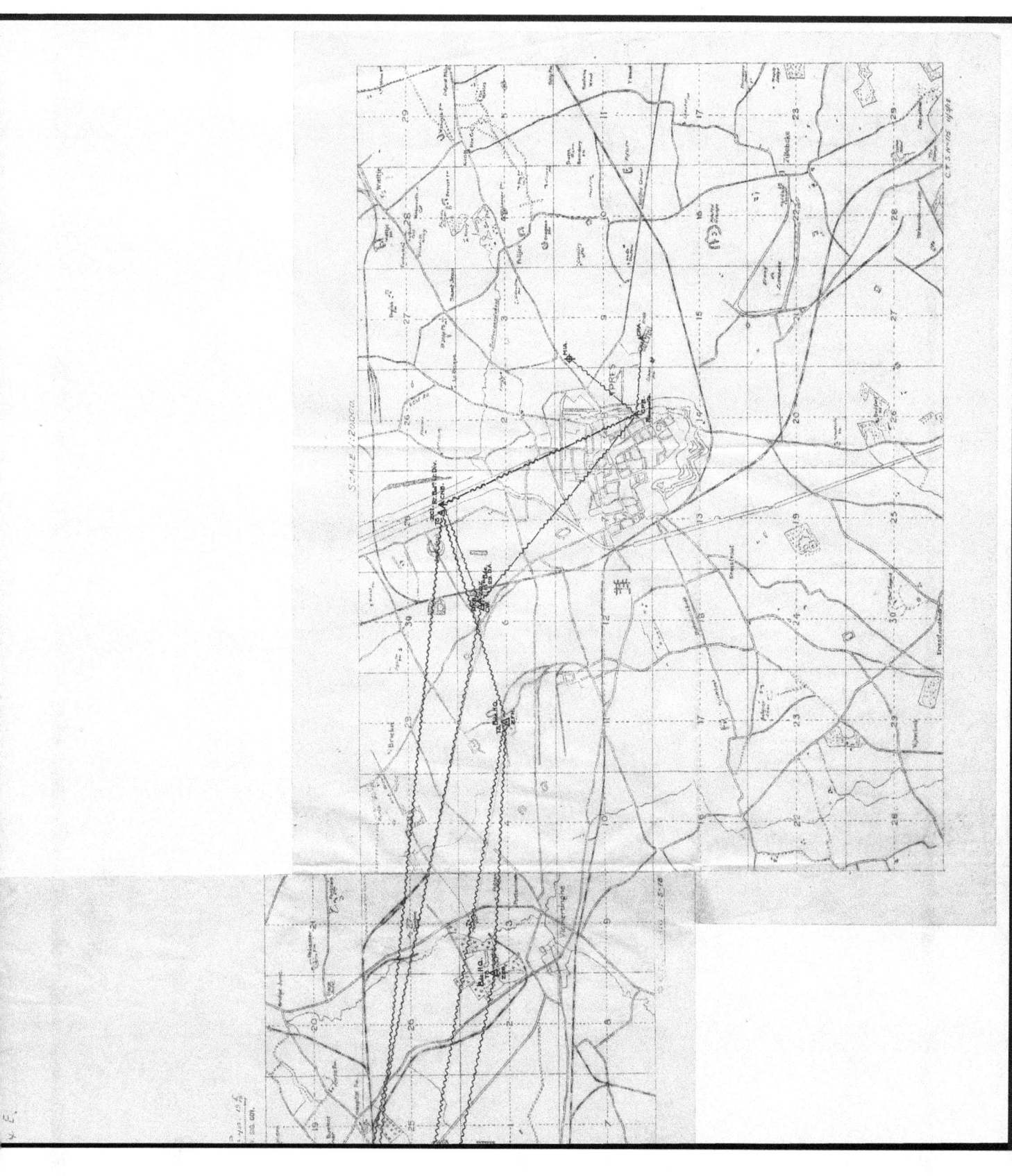

Appendix. E.

Appendix F.

WM 132   May 12 - 18

O C
41 Div Sig Co

Sir
          Herewith please find first ten days
Syllabus for BB & Amplifier Class

                          H. Stanwell Lieut
                            i/c Wireless
                            41 Div Sig Co

Syllabus for PB & Amplifier Class

	A.M. Morning	**P.M. Afternoon**
Monday	9 – 10.30 Buzzer Tests 10.30 to 12.30 Connecting up PB and Amplifier & Laying Lines	2–3 Lecture { Conductors Insulators { Potential Action of Cell { Capacity 3–4 Procedure
Tuesday	9–0 to 12.30 } Short distance Outside Work & Earths. PB & Amplifier	2–3 2nd Lecture { Magnets & Magnetic Substances { Magnetic Field & Strain { Magnetic Induction 3–4 Buzzer Practice
Wednesday	9–0 to 12.30 } Outdoor (Earths Work & Faults)	2–3 3rd Lecture { Construction & Action of { PB 3–4 Buzzer Practice
Thursday	9–0 to 12.30 } Outdoor Work, PB & Amp to PB & Amp	2–3 4th Lecture { Simple Explanation of { Electron Theory Valves { Amplifier 3–4 Buzzer Practice
Friday	9–0 to 12.30 } Outside Work Two PB to One Amplifier	2–3 5th Lecture – Accumulators 3–4 Buzzer Practice
Saturday	9–0 to 12.30 } Outdoor Long distance Work	Written Paper
Monday	9–0 to 12.30 } Outdoor Long distance Work	2–3 6th Lecture { Map Reading, Protractor { & Compass 3–4 Working out Angles
Tuesday	9–0 to 12.30 } Outdoor Work	2–3 Recapitulation of PB & Earths 3–4 Buzzer Practice
Wednesday	9–0 to 12.30 } Outdoor Work	Tests

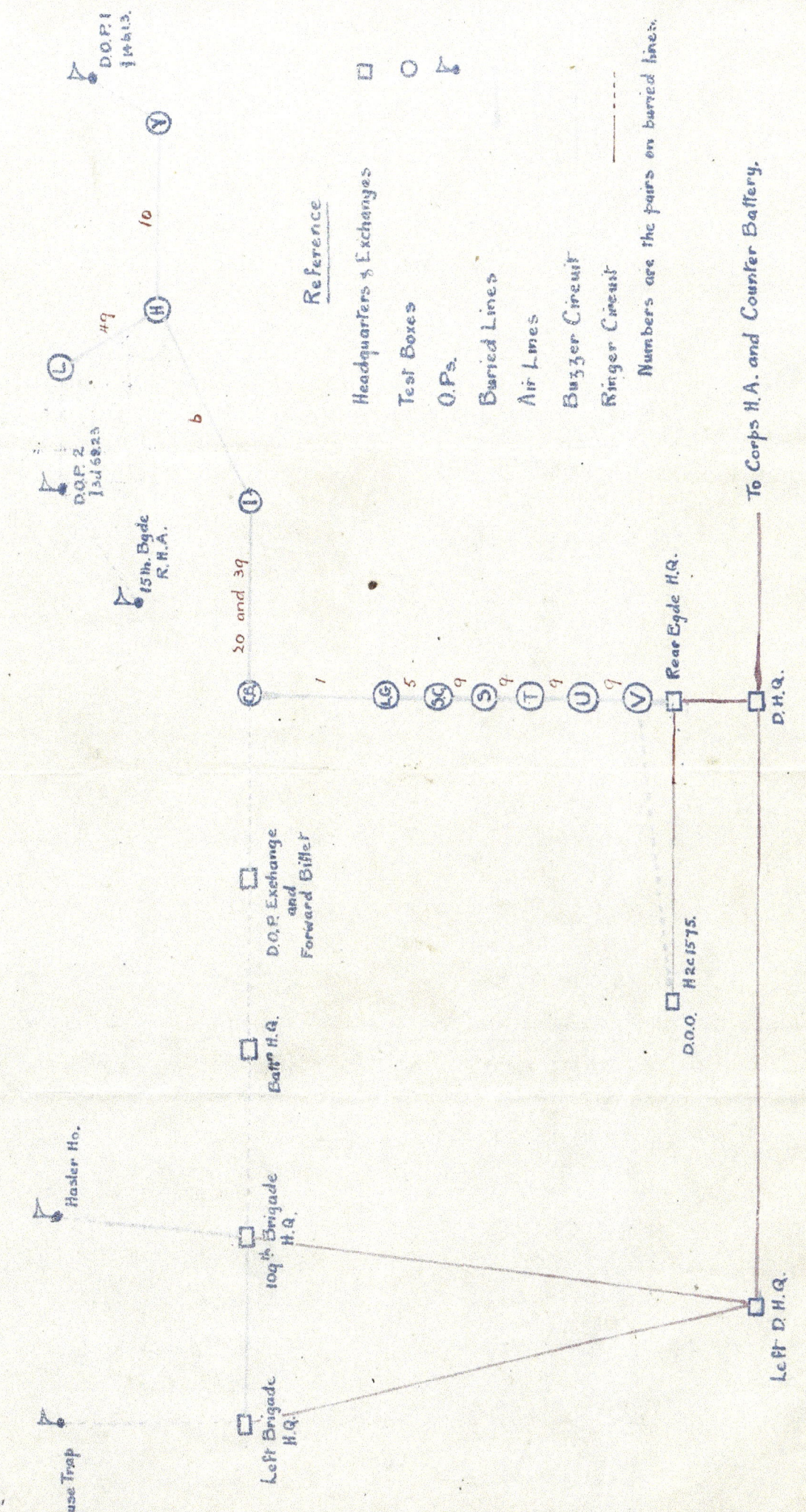

Appendix. J.

41st Divisional Defence Scheme

Communications.

Wire Communications.

1. Between Division and Brigades.

Forward of Divl. H/Q. Communications run to Brigades by buried cables, ground lines, and air lines.

A buried cable route runs from Divl. H/Q to A 26 a.9.5, thence by overground cable partly in the canal to C.D. in B 25.a. vide Map. A., thence by old buried cable to Machine Gun Farm. This is the safest route.

Four Air line and Ground Cable routes, well separated, run to S.D. in H. 2 c. 8.9 and thence forward all lines with the exception of locals are buried.

The forward buries are old but have been restored as far as time and labour permit, and may be considered as proof to a direct hit from guns up to a calibre of 4.2"

2. The two Brigades holding the line with H/Q at Machine Gun Farm about H 5. Central are connected to their battalions by four separate routes all buried cable. vide Map. A.

The buries are maintained by an area party with H/Q at Vlamertinghe Chateau and by Divisional Linemen in test boxes at important junctions

The Royal Artillery, Machine Gun Battalion and the Divl. Observation officer all have lines on the Divl. buried system.

Wireless and Power Buzzer Communications.

A complete Wireless chain is working from Divl. H/Q to Battns in the front line vide Map B.

A Wilson set at D.H.Q. works to a transmitting Trench set at Reserve Bde H/Q Mamertinghe Chateau, thence to a second Trench set at the H/Q of the two Brigades in the line at Machine Gun Farm, thence forward a Power Buzzer and Amplifier Station works to Reigersburg H.6.6. central, thence to a station in the Ypres ramparts in I 8 d 1.3 thence to two other Battn. H/Q in I 9 c 5.2 and I 9 a 2.7.

Lateral wireless communication also exists to flank Divisions, flank Brigades and flank Battalions vide Map B. attached.

Visual Communications.

Visual communication has been tested through and can be used in case of emergency between Lovie Chateau and Mamertinghe Chateau, thence to Machine Gun Farm, thence to Ypres ramparts. In the forward areas Visual communication is working from the ramparts I 8 d 1.5 to the Battn at the Ecole I 9 c 1.5, thence to the Battn about I 9 a 1.9, thence to a Battn of the Division on our left at I 3 a 9.9.

Messenger Dogs.

One group of messenger dogs is allotted to each Bde. in the line, and this provides an alternate means of communication between the Battns and H/Qs of the Bdes.

Pigeons.

Pigeons are allotted as follows:—

8 Birds daily to each Brigade in the line
6   do   do to the Divisional Observation Officer.
4   do   do to the R.A.

May. 1918.

41 D Signals
10.2.26

Army Form C. 2118.

WAR DIARY
or
INTELLIGENCE SUMMARY.
(Erase heading not required.)

Place	Date	Hour	Summary of Events and Information	Remarks and references to Appendices
LOVIE CHATEAU	1/8		O.C. Signals 49th Divn was shown round the line and the existing system of communications explained to him.	
	2/8		Linesmen of the 49th Divn Signal Co. are in position in the lines named by our linesmen.	
	3/8		U by at ROME FARM was hit & set on fire by an incendiary shell. An important entry of communication was therefore cut, which was unfortunate as the relief by O/C Sigs 49 Divn was in progress. Owing to ROME FARM burning all day, it was impossible to put the U route through, but 2 extra lines were allotted to us by O.C. Sigs 36 Divn, who was most helpful in every way, and who worked in the street Maison. O.C. Sigs 49 Divn took over the communications at 6 p.m.	
	4/8		The Signal Coy moved by march & rail route to NIEURLET in accordance with 41st Divn Signal Coy Order No. 38 vide Appendix A attached. Capt W.McC. Petrich left the Coy to take up an appt as O/C Sig Australian Heavy Artillery.	Appdx A

Army Form C. 2118.

WAR DIARY
INTELLIGENCE SUMMARY.
(Erase heading not required.)

Instructions regarding War Diaries and Intelligence Summaries are contained in F. S. Regs., Part II. and the Staff Manual respectively. Title pages will be prepared in manuscript.

Place	Date	Hour	Summary of Events and Information	Remarks and references to Appendices
LOUIE CHATEAU	4/6/18		Lt. Col. Parres left the Coy, and reserved to command No. 2 Secn on his appointment as Signal Instructor at the Signal Base, ABBEVILLE.	
NIEURLET	5/6/18		O.C. Signals visited D.D. Sigs at Army H.Q. with reference to the appointment of Officers to the Signal Co. The Genl. Staff were asked to instruct Brigades to form Brigade forward parties. This was done vide Appendix B. attached.	Appdx. B
	6/18		Training commenced. All cable wagons are out cable laying and the "stepping up" was practised by the wireless stations.	
	7/6/18		Divl. H.Q. and the Divl. Signal Co. moved to GIVENCHY CHATEAU, EPERLECQUES in accordance with Divl. Signal Co. Order No. 39 vide Appendix C. attached	Apdx C.
EPERLECQUES	8/6/18		Day spent by Coy settling down "cleaning up". O.C. Sigs visited Signal School & inspected the new class of Infantry Art'y which joined up on the 7th of June.	

Army Form C. 2118.

WAR DIARY
INTELLIGENCE SUMMARY.
(Erase heading not required.)

Instructions regarding War Diaries and Intelligence Summaries are contained in F. S. Regs., Part II. and the Staff Manual respectively. Title pages will be prepared in manuscript.

Place	Date	Hour	Summary of Events and Information	Remarks and references to Appendices
EPERLECQUES	9/7/8		Rest day. Nothing to report	
	10/7/8		Training performed. Cable Wagon work, Visual Signalling & Mobile wireless being practised. A buzz reading class for NCOs was also started.	
	11/7/8		Training continued as on the 10th. 2 Lt E.R Lusk joined the Signal Co. from 28th Div Detachment and was appointed to command No 2. Sec. in place of Lt pro Purves at Abbeville	
	12/6/8		Training continued.	
	13/6/8		Training continued. Capt. D. Portway joined the Signal Co from 1st Army Signal School as 2d in Command vice Capt. Patrick.	
	14/7/8 15/6/8		Training continued.	

Army Form C. 2118.

WAR DIARY
INTELLIGENCE SUMMARY.
(Erase heading not required.)

Place	Date	Hour	Summary of Events and Information	Remarks and references to Appendices
EPERLECQUES	16/8		Nothing to report. 2nd Lt. Dyke joined from the Machine Gun Corps Base Depot & was posted to command No 5 Sec of the Coy.	
	17/8		Training continued. A crusade is now being carried on in order to induce Staff Officers to write their telegrams in accordance with Army OB.1280. This is meeting with success.	
	18/8		123 Infy Bde carried out an attack practice in which the Signal Coy cooperated both from a point of view of Divisional lines, and the use of Bde Forward Parties in open warfare. Very valuable lessons were learnt vide appendix D. Signal Coy Orders No X. and Appendix E. Notes on the lessons learnt.	Appdx D do E
	19/8		Training cont'd	
	20/8		122 Infy Bde carried out an attack practice through the FOREST of EPERLECQUES. Signals worked very satisfactorily and valuable lessons were learnt vide Appendix F.	Appdx F.

Army Form C. 2118.

WAR DIARY
or
INTELLIGENCE SUMMARY.
(Erase heading not required.)

Instructions regarding War Diaries and Intelligence Summaries are contained in F. S. Regs., Part II. and the Staff Manual respectively. Title pages will be prepared in manuscript.

Place	Date	Hour	Summary of Events and Information	Remarks and references to Appendices
EPERLECQUES	20/6		Signal Coy Orders No X 2. and Appendix G Notes on the lessons learnt	Apple G.
	21-22/6		Training continued.	
	23/6		Training continued. Orders received from 2d Army that Capt Scott Moncrieff is appointed 2d in command of the Signal Coy from 25th Divl Sig Co. vice Capt Portway.	
	24/6		Warning orders received of the move of the Divn to relieve the 7th French Divn in the line in the SCHERPENBERG Sector	
	25/6		Nothing to report.	
	26/6		Company moved to OUDEZEELE by march and bus route vide Appendix H Att'd. The Divn is now in Reserve to the 14th French Corps.	Apple H
OUDEZEELE	27/6		Signal Coy Officers made a preliminary reconnaissance of communications in the	

Army Form C. 2118.

WAR DIARY
INTELLIGENCE SUMMARY.
(Erase heading not required.)

Instructions regarding War Diaries and Intelligence Summaries are contained in F. S. Regs., Part II. and the Staff Manual respectively. Title pages will be prepared in manuscript.

Place	Date	Hour	Summary of Events and Information	Remarks and references to Appendices
OUDEZEELE	27/6		Area of the 7th French Div. whom we have orders to relieve at 3 a.m. on the 2nd July.	
	28/6		Nothing to report	
	29/6		A percentage of Linemen are now attached to the 7th French Div. for purpose of acquainting themselves with the lines. All lines in the new area are overground and the buried cable system will have to be started at the first available opportunity.	
	30/6		Forward Parties assembled at the 51st Signal School, RUBROUCK vide Appendix I attached, which was sent out by O/C Signals through the General Staff	Appendix I

R.W. Ackerman Major
O/C Signals 41st Div.

Army Form C. 2118.

WAR DIARY
or
INTELLIGENCE SUMMARY.
(Erase heading not required.)

Instructions regarding War Diaries and Intelligence Summaries are contained in F. S. Regs., Part II. and the Staff Manual respectively. Title pages will be prepared in manuscript.

Place	Date	Hour	Summary of Events and Information	Remarks and references to Appendices
	2/8		3 ORs arrived from Base Signal Depot	
	3/8		1 OR reported from Hospital.	
	5/8		Capt. W. H. Pollock left the Coy for the Russian Corps Attrny B.E.F. May Sig Co. Lt. Jee Power left the Coy for temporary duty at the Signal Base Depot.	
			18 ORs left the Coy for duty with Capt. Pollock & 1 OR for duty with L. Power.	
			1 OR lent to Can. R.A.F.	
	6/8		2 Offrs & 2 ORs mentioned in Despatches. 1 OR awarded D.C.M.	
			1 OR wounded Acc. C. Thompson awarded M.C. 1 OR M.S.M. 1 OR D.C.M.	
	9/8		1 OR rejoined from Base Signal Depot	
	11/8		2 ORs " " " "	
			Bdr. Pottery arrived from the Army Signal School with 1 OR to O'Rush " " 2nd Area Bar'	
	14/8		1 OR rejoined from Base Signal Depot	
	17/8		2 Lt Byfe WP arrived from M.C. Base & took over command of No 5 Sect.	
	18		1 OR evacuated to Hospital	
	19		2 ORs arrived 1 from Base Signal Depot & 1 from M.G. B.M.	
	20		1 OR admitted to Hospital Wounded.	
	24		Capt. Portney left the Coy for E Army with 1 OR. 2 ORs arrived from Base Signal Depot	
	26		2 ORs evacuated to 2d Aust CCS	

M. W. Shannon Maj
OC Signals 4th Divn

MSS 266.

Appendix A

41st Signal Coy Order
No. 38

(i) The Signal Company will move to NIEURLET on 4 June 1918.

(ii) The horse transport & mounted personnel will march at 5:30 a.m. under Lt. JEFFERIES. Route: HOUTKERQUE — WORMHOUDT — RUBROUCK — BROXEELE. A two hours halt will be made about midday, & care will be taken that the road is kept clear during the halt.

(iii) Dismounted personnel under Lt. STANWORTH M. will entrain at PROVEN at 12:00. Troops will be at the entraining point at ~~9:00~~ 11:00.

(iv) ~~Motor transport will move to NIEURLET leaving~~

(IV) It [will?] and arrange [re?]
[...] supplies direct with
the supply officer

(V) Rations will be taken
by the troops [...] by rail

(VI) The storm [...] lorry will
leave LOVIE at 7 am on the
[...] with instruments and
personnel for first office
relief.

(VII) Actual office closes LOVIE
11 am & reopens NIEURLET
same hour

(VIII) The Box car is at the
disposal of Capt Patrick and
Lt PURVES who will arrange
that it is back at
LOVIE CHAU at 10.30 am
for carriage of stores
to NIEURLET

(IX) Acknowledge

[signature]
Major
[...]

3/6/15

Copy No 1   O
         2   Capt Patrick
         3   Lt Jefferies
         4   Lt Stammers
         5   CSM
         6   CQMS
         7   Sgt Cockburn
         8   File
         9   Diary

Appendix. B

41st Div.
G. 426.
34/4.

122nd Infantry Brigade.
123rd Infantry Brigade.
124th Infantry Brigade.
41st Divl. Signal Coy.
"Q".

1.— G.O's.C. Infantry Brigades will assemble their Brigade Forward Parties forthwith.

2.— Arrangement will be made by Brigades for these parties to live together and to train under the Brigade Forward Party officers. The training will be supervised by the Brigade Signalling officers.

3.— Training will be carried out as laid down in S.S.191 "Intercommunication in the Field", Sections 9 and 11.

4.— Brigade Forward Parties will consist of the following :—

"A" Detachment.
  1 Officer.
  10 Runners.(these will not be trained signallers).
  1 N.C.O. and 6 Visual Signallers.
  4 Pigeon men.

  Total:— 1 Officer, 1 N.C.O., 20 men.

"B" Detachment.
  1 Officer.
  1 N.C.O. and 8 O.R's. Telephone detachment.
  1 N.C.O. and 4 O.R's. For Power Buzzer.

  Total:— 1 Officer, 2 N.C.O's., 12 men.

Reserve: 2 N.C.O's.
         8 Runners (not Signallers).
         8 Signallers.

GRAND TOTAL: 2 Officers.
              5 N.C.O's.
              48 men.

5.— The Amplifier men with the Divisional Signal Company and their instruments will be available on demand to O.C. 41st Divl. Signal Coy. when required.
The following equipment will be required by the Brigade Forward Parties :—

  3 Lucas Lamps.
  3 pairs Binoculars.
  12 Small White Signal Flags.
  8 Telephones. D.III.
  Cable, on small ½ mile drums.
  Power Buzzers, 2 per Brigade.
  Amplifiers, 1 per Brigade.(on demand from
                                O.C. Signals).
  1 Aeroplane Ground Sheet.
  Stationery.

Brigades will arrange to draw from Battalions any extra equipment they may require to make up the above.

5th June, 1918.

Lieut.Colonel,
General Staff.

Appendix. C

HSS268

41 Divl Signal Coy Order
No 39

(1) The Signal Coy will march today to EPERLECQUES under LT STANWORTH. M.C.
Time of start 12·30 PM
ROUTE   ST MOMELIN – LE BAS – SERQUES – MOULLE – HOULLE.

(2) The motor lorry will move under instructions from CQMS & also the Box car under orders of LT STANWORTH

(3) Dismounted personnel will march with the coy. Dress, drill order with rifles arrangements will be made by CSM to carry their kits.

(4) Signal office closes NIEURLET 4·30 PM reopens EPERLECQUES same hour. Sergt COCKBURN will arrange office reliefs.

7/6/18

Appendix. D.

SECRET.   Copy No. 6.

123RD INFANTRY BRIGADE SCHEME ON 18TH JUNE 1918.

41ST DIVISIONAL SIGNAL COY. ORDER No. X.

Ref. Map. Hazebrouck 5a. 1/40,000 and Sheet 27a.S.E. 1/20,000.

(1)   German force is advancing in the direction from DUNKERQUE to ST OMER and a detachment estimated at 2 Battns halted about POLINCOVE last night.

(2)   The 123rd Infantry Brigade will assemble about TATINGHAM at 9-15 a.m. and will move to establish itself on the high ground between GRAND DIFQUES and MORINGHEM.

(3)   The advance to be carried out in successive bounds.
The 1st to the line - N.6.a.1.8. - W.4.a.7.4. - W.3.d.6.3. - W.2.c.7.3.
The 2nd to the line - Q.33.b.9.7. - Q.32.c.0.0.
The 3rd to the line - Q.27.a.0.3. - Q.25.d.3.0.

(4)   Divisional H.Qrs will be established at Road Junction in LONGUENESSE X.15.b.7.7. at 9 a.m.
Wire and Wireless communication will be established between Divl. H.Qrs and Bde H.Qrs at X.7.c.3.7. by 9-10 a.m.

(5)   Capt. Portway will arrange to follow the Bde H.Qrs on the move with a cable wagon from L.B. detachment and Lt.Stanworth will arrange to keep Bde H.Qrs on the move in touch with D.H.Q. by means of "stepping up" wireless stations.

(6)   Please acknowledge.

                                          Major.,
17th June 1918.   O.C. 41st Divl. Signal Coy. R.E.

        Copy No. 1.   "G" 41st Division.
                2.   Staff, 123rd Inf.Bde.
                3.   O.C.Sigs. -do-
                4.   Capt. Portway.
                5.   Lt. Stanworth.
                6.   O.C. Signals. ✓
                7.   Diary.

Appendix E.

HSS 288

To O/C No 3 Secⁿ 41st Div^l Signal Co R.E.
H/Qs 123 Inf Bde (for information).

Notes on Signal Scheme carried out on
18th June 1918.

(1) Always establish a Signal Office at once at each halt. Mark it with a Signal flag in a conspicuous position.
It should fulfil the following conditions
(a) Be on or near a main road.
(b) Be close to staff.
(c) Be in a central position for Cable, Wireless and Visual stations.

(2) Directly Office is formed all orderlies must know the way to Div. Cable wagon, Div. Wireless station and Brigade Cable and Visual stations.

(3) Wire to Sigs Divⁿ all moves of Bde H/Q & forecasts of moves, giving as much notice as possible.

(4) Your forward party was too far back at the start & should have moved up just in rear of main guard.

H.S.S. 288.

(4) The forward party must also be in a central position. It was rather on a flank and a long way from H/Q 10th R.W. Kent Regt.

(5) Worry your Staff to get early information of all moves, and get a ruling from them as to the disposal of messages arriving at the Signal Office, when no member of the Staff is present.

E. Hotchkiss
Major

19/6/18.   O/C. 41st Div'l Signal Co. R.E.

Appendix. 7.

Copy No. 7

41ST DIVISIONAL SIGNAL COY. ORDER NO. X.2.

19th June 1918.

Ref. Sheet. 1/40,000. 27a. East Half.

(1) The advance of the 41st Division Eastward through EPERLECQUES FOREST will be continued to-morrow.

(2) The 122nd Infantry Brigade will be in position at 9-30 a.m. on the front K.11.b.0.2 - K.17.b.5.2.
Brigade H.Q. will be in position at bend of road K.18.b.9.6 at 9-30 a.m.

(3) Divisional H.Q. will be established at WATTEN DAM in L.8.c.6.4. at 9-30 a.m.

(4) Lieut. JEFFERIES with a cable wagon and limber from 1.A. Cable Section will establish wire communication between Divl. and Bde H.Q. by 9-30 a.m. He will be prepared to follow up Bde H.Q. when they move and keep them in constant wire communication with Division.

(5) Lieut. STANWORTH will arrange to establish Wireless Communication between D.H.Q. and H.Q. 122nd Infantry Bde. Communication to be through by 9-30 a.m. Lieut. STANWORTH will follow any movements of Bde H.Q. by "stepping up" wireless stations so as to keep them in constant wireless communication with Divl. H.Q.

ACKNOWLEDGE.

O.C.
COMMANDING 41st DIV. SIG. COY.

Issued to Signals 12 noon.

Copy No. 1. 122nd Inf. Bde H.Q.
2. O.C. Sigs. 122nd Inf Bde.
3. O.C. Signals.
4. Lieut. Jefferies.
5. Lieut. Stanworth.
6. "G" 41st Div.
7. Diary.

Appendix "G"

Copy No. 5

NOTES ON SIGNAL COMMUNICATIONS 122ND INFANTRY BRIGADE
SCHEME CARRIED OUT 20TH JUNE 1918.

(1) During the 1st phase of the operations the Brigade Forward Party was not in it's correct position; being K.17.b.7.6. and not K.11.d.6.2. as ordered. It is very important to have the Brigade Forward Station in a central position and in the above case the Forward party was a long distance from the K.R.R. H.Q.

(2) In open warfare the question of using lines forward of Bde. H.Q. will depend on circumstances. It may be assumed that during open fighting in normal country, lines will not be laid and the communication between Forward Parties and Brigade H.Q. will consist of Visual, Power Buzzer, D.R. and sometimes wireless.

In case of a specific action, with a limited objective or in a country which is manifestly unsuited to visual signalling, the Staff should instruct the Brigade Signalling Officer to lay cables, it being always born in mind that an Infantry Brigade only carries 8 miles of cable and that the question of the supply of cable in open warfare is one of extreme difficulty. It will rarely be advisable to lay cables from the Brigade forward party to Battn. H.Q., but this again must be left to the discretion of the Staff concerned.

(3) When time is of great importance, as is often the case in open warfare, the Staff will, if they think fit, send wireless messages in "clear"; in this case the words "in clear" will be written in space Z of the message form signed by a Staff Officer.

Messages in clear must never be sent in practice schemes.

(4) Too much reliance is still being placed on Telephone Communication and communication is sometimes considered as broken down except by orderly, even when Power Buzzer, Visual and Wireless Communications are through.

During open warfare the telephone must be considered as an abnormal rather than a normal means of communication.

20th June 1918.

O.C. 41st Divl. Signal Coy. R.E.

Copy No.1. "G" 41st Division.
       2. H.Q. 122nd Inf.Bde.
       3. O.C. Signs. -do-
       4. File.
       5. Diary.

Appendix H

HS5299

41st Divl Signal Coy
Order No 40

(I) Horse transport under Lt Jefferies will march to OUDEZEELE at 7 am tomorrow.
Route WATTEN – GAZEMBERG – WEMERS – CAPPEL.
They will not pass LEDERZEELE STN until 124 Inf Bde group is clear.

(II) The motor transport (less the light lorry) will leave at 6 am & proceed direct to OUDEZEELE by most direct route under Lt Stanworth.

(III) Lt Sylvester will open the office at OUDEZEELE at 12 noon.

(IV) Lt Dykes will supervise the embussing of the dismounted personnel.

Appendix H. cont.

V. All motor transport with the exception of the electric light lorry, will return to EPERLECQUES as soon as possible from OUDEZEELE for carriage of remaining stores & personnel.

VI. The electric light lorry will leave for LEDEZEELE at 9 am.

(VII) A table wagon with detachment complete will report to Capt Cranshaw at WATOU CH at 6 PM

VIII. Q will place one lorry at the disposal of the Signal Coy for transport of dismounted personnel at 6 am tomorrow

IX acknowledge.

Crundtenni, Maj.

25/6/16.

COMMANDING 51st DIV SIG. COY.

Appendix. J.

41st Div.
G.762
(54/4).

122nd Infantry Brigade.
123rd Infantry Brigade.
124th Infantry Brigade.
41st Divl. Signal Coy. 2.

1. Brigade Forward Parties will be concentrated at the Divisional Signal School, HURROUCK on the 30th inst. Transport arrangements will be notified by "Q".

2. Training will be continued under supervision of Commandant 41st Divl Signal School.

3. The following equipment will be sent by each Brigade :-

   2 D.III telephones.
   1 Lucas Lamp.
   As many small flags as possible, up to 1 per man.

4. All ranks will be rationed for the 30th Instant. They will be taken on to the ration strength of the Signal School from the 1st July inclusive. Officers will bring their messing utensils and will mess in the Signal School Officer's Mess.

5. The object of bringing the Brigade Forward Parties together out of the line is to complete their training and to render them a perfect instrument should the Division be engaged in active operations.
   It is hoped that the Forward Parties will be kept up to establishment but the G.Os.C. Infantry Brigades can exchange tired Signal personnel from the Battns in the line for fresh men from the Brigade Forward Parties should they so desire.
   In case of emergency, reinforcements to replace casualties in Battn Signallers may be drawn from the Brigade Forward Parties under training, but this will not be done if it can be avoided.

6. Nominal Rolls of personnel of the Forward Parties proceeding to the Divisional Signal School will be forwarded to O.C. Signals 41st Division by first D.R. on 29th inst and a copy sent to this office.
   The 124th Infantry Brigade need not send an officer with their Brigade Forward Party until their Brigade Signalling officer returns from leave.

28th June, 1918.

E.A.Beck.
Lieut-Colonel,
General Staff.

On His Majesty's Service

Hl. Div. "A"

SECRET

War Diary.

41 D Signals
Vol 27

July 18

4

SECRET

Army Form C. 2118.

WAR DIARY
of
INTELLIGENCE SUMMARY.
(Erase heading not required.)

Instructions regarding War Diaries and Intelligence Summaries are contained in F. S. Regs., Part II and the Staff Manual respectively. Title pages will be prepared in manuscript.

Place	Date	Hour	Summary of Events and Information	Remarks and references to Appendices
OUDEZEELE	1/7/16		The necessary personnel of the Signal Co moved to LA LINGE 300 yds N of ABEELE at 10 p.m. and started to relieve Signals of the 7th French Div.	
Le LINGE	2/7/16		Signals relief complete 3 a.m. An excellent relief in every way in spite of difficulties caused by the difference of organization of British and French Divisions, and to the great number of exchanges which the French always use in their system of communications. There are only their cable lines from Divisional to the front line. The French system was taken over with as few changes as possible in accordance with the instructions at Appendix A. There was some trouble with the machine guns relief owing to the Machine Gunners changing their M.G. 3 times and their units not knowing where to go. 1 am much annoyed that the formation of a No 5 Coy, for Squad Co in unnecessary and a mistake.	Apdx A.
	3/7/16		Routes for Divisional Buried Cable in conjunction with Corps Buried Cable system were reconnoitred and related in accordance with tracing in the Appendix B attached.	Apdx B.
	4/7/16		The Divisional Sector is at present fairly quiet and the open cable system	

Army Form C. 2118.

WAR DIARY
-or-
INTELLIGENCE SUMMARY.
(Erase heading not required.)

Place	Date	Hour	Summary of Events and Information	Remarks and references to Appendices
LE LINGE	4/7/18		routes are being reconnoitred in front around at Wierinck. Wireless in working entirety in accordance with diagram made Attention C attached, and the Visual System is also in order in accordance with Appendix D attached.	Major C as D
	5/7/18		Preparations were made to start burying cable on the night of 6/7 with a *covering party of* 400 men made up as follows. R.A. 100 am. each Infantry Bttn 100	
	6/7/18		Divisional Buried Cable route started at 10pm from 13.d.18.0 Sheet 28 NW.	
	7/7/18		Divl H/Q moved to a hut camp at K.29.c.3.2 Sheet 28	
Hut Camp @ K.29.c.3.2 Sheet 28 N.1.	8/7/18		The cable burying is not progressing as reliably as I before owing to difficulties with the working parties.	
	9/7/18		A silent day. No wire communication being used at all and wires of Division. The Huns have not answered at all and the evening will take to not to be an *easy* move.	

D.D. & L. London E.C
(1050a) Wt W.3300/P713 750,000 3/18 E 688 Forms/C2118/16.

Army Form C. 2118.

WAR DIARY
INTELLIGENCE SUMMARY.
(Erase heading not required.)

Place	Date	Hour	Summary of Events and Information	Remarks and references to Appendices
Har(condr)	9/8		As required in the system of numbering the Divl Wireless Stations by the higher formation. American Signallers were attached to the Company and distributed as follows:	
			4 per Battn. ... 36	
			4 " Brigade ... 12	
			15 " H/Q No 1 Sec — 15	
			— 63	
	10/8		A very good cable burying party last night, and the buried cable is more thorough to M5a15, buried everywhere to a depth of 6ft.	
	11/8		Work on buried cable continuing.	
	12/8		do	
	13/8		do	
			There are rumours of an early enemy attack on this front. The lorry has now reached the H/Qrs of the 123 Bde, and will be connected up to Division as far as this Brigade is concerned, as soon as the Corps Bury links up with the Divl Cable Head.	

Army Form C. 2118.

WAR DIARY
or
INTELLIGENCE SUMMARY.
(Erase heading not required.)

Instructions regarding War Diaries and Intelligence Summaries are contained in F. S. Regs., Part II. and the Staff Manual respectively. Title pages will be prepared in manuscript.

Place	Date	Hour	Summary of Events and Information	Remarks and references to Appendices
HUT CAMP	14/2/18		An overground line from Rene Test Box was laid to the word in MI Od road to be ready in case the 124 Bde H/Q moved back from the SCHERPENBERG TUNNELS in a hurry.	
	15/2/18		Owing to progress in the buried cable work it was possible this day to change the system of communications. In place of the old French system of overground lines, all 3 Brigades are now connected with the AA Test Box. 124 Brigade being connected by overground wires from this point. This is a great economy in personnel.	
	16/2/18		A hostile attack was considered imminent, and all working parties were stopped in the Div'l Area, with the exception of the Cable Burying party. All linemen's posts were manned, and wireless communication taken through at frequent intervals during the day & night.	
	17/2/18		Cable Burying continued.	
	19/2/18		A second party of American personnel reported, and were sent out to Brigades Batteries.	
	20/2/18		Cable Burying continued. The Burry is now complete to 122. 123 Inf/y Bdes.	

Army Form C. 2118.

WAR DIARY
INTELLIGENCE SUMMARY.
(Erase heading not required.)

Place	Date	Hour	Summary of Events and Information	Remarks and references to Appendices
HUT CAMP	20/7/18		This includes their liaison lines to the Artillery.	
	21/7/18		The Divl Forward Exchange was changed from INTER to A.C.D. G.25.d.4.6. The following lines were put down through from Rearwn to the two above mentioned Brigades, and the air/two personnel withdrawn from the Forward Exchange to Rearcoart H/Q.	
	22/7/23 7/18		Cable Burying continued	
	24/7/8		Very little work was done Cable Burying, owing to a Batln of the 123 Infy Brigade arriving at the Rendezvous without Tools.	
	25/7/18		Buried Cable reached the 124 Bde H.Q. in road nr M10.d about 12 midnight (26/7/18)	
	26/7/18		The Buried cable was bombed during the night between 2N and AA Bties and Bde Brigades Appendix E	Appendix E
	27/7/18		The Enemy shows on the hired wire between A.A.Bty and the SCHERPENBERG was unaccounted atating from the forward area. 40 men working by day and under O.C.R.E. S.A.Div SCHERPENBERG and 200 men at night in three shifts working on line position.	

Army Form C. 2118.

WAR DIARY
or
INTELLIGENCE SUMMARY.
(Erase heading not required.)

Place	Date	Hour	Summary of Events and Information	Remarks and references to Appendices
HUT CAMP	28/7/18		Work on the Buzy continued.	
	29/7/18		American Wireless Personnel went attached to the Division as officers and 2 O.R.S	
	30/7/18		The Divisional Buried Cable system completed in accordance with Route Diagram attached hereto Appendix E.	Appendix E
	31/7/18		4th course at the Div.l Signal School completed. Return of R&R Signallers in the Division at this date is as follows:	

	122 Inf Bde		123 Inf Bde		124 Inf Bde	
	Offrs	O.R.S	Offrs	O.R.S	Offrs	O.R.S
Signallers trained	5	144	11	177	7	174
" " under training		26		50		55

The Brigade Armed Parties are still under training at the Div.l Signal School and have reached a high state of efficiency.

Map Appendix A shows the Communications as taken over from the Division on the 2nd July 1918. Appendix E – Diagram Appendix G-H shows the complete Route Diagram Appendix E + H shows the complete Communications by Cable, Visual, Wireless and P/O as they exist on this date.

Appendix A
Appx H
Gt A

S.C. Signals 41 Div

WAR DIARY
— or —
INTELLIGENCE SUMMARY.
(Erase heading not required.)

Army Form C. 2118.

Place	Date	Hour	Summary of Events and Information	Remarks and references to Appendices
Le LINGE	2/7/18		1 OR reported from C.C.S. 1 OR evacuated sick by shell fire	
	4/7/18		1 OR " " " 4 ORs joined from Base Signal Depôt	
	10/7/18		Capt Reynolds arrived from 19 Corps Wireless with 1 OR to Bethmann Capt. Scott Hammond arrived from 25 Div with 1 OR as servant. 1 OR joined from Base Depôt	
			One OR left Coy to be attached to 223 Siege Batt R.G.A.	
	12/7/18		Capt Reynolds & 1 OR sent to 19 Corps	
	13/7/18		Capt Purcell RE on loan 19 " . 1 OR evacuated to C.C.S.	
	19/7/18		2 ORs evacuated to C.C.S.	
	20/7/18		Capt Purcell left the Coy for the 6th Div Sig Co. 1 OR evacuated to base	
	23/7/18		2 ORs join 1 ORs sent to The Coy. 1 Reinforcement arrived from 66 Div Sig Co as despatch rider	
			1 OR arrived attached from attached to coy	
	25/7/18		1 OR arrived from base Signal Depôt	
	27/7/18		1 OR " " " "	
	29/7/18		2 ORs " " " "	
	31/7/18		4 " " " "	

Kenneth McLennan Major
OC Signals 41 Divn.

Appendix B.

DIAGRAM
of proposed bury
Shts 28 N.W. & S.W.
Scale $\frac{1}{20000}$

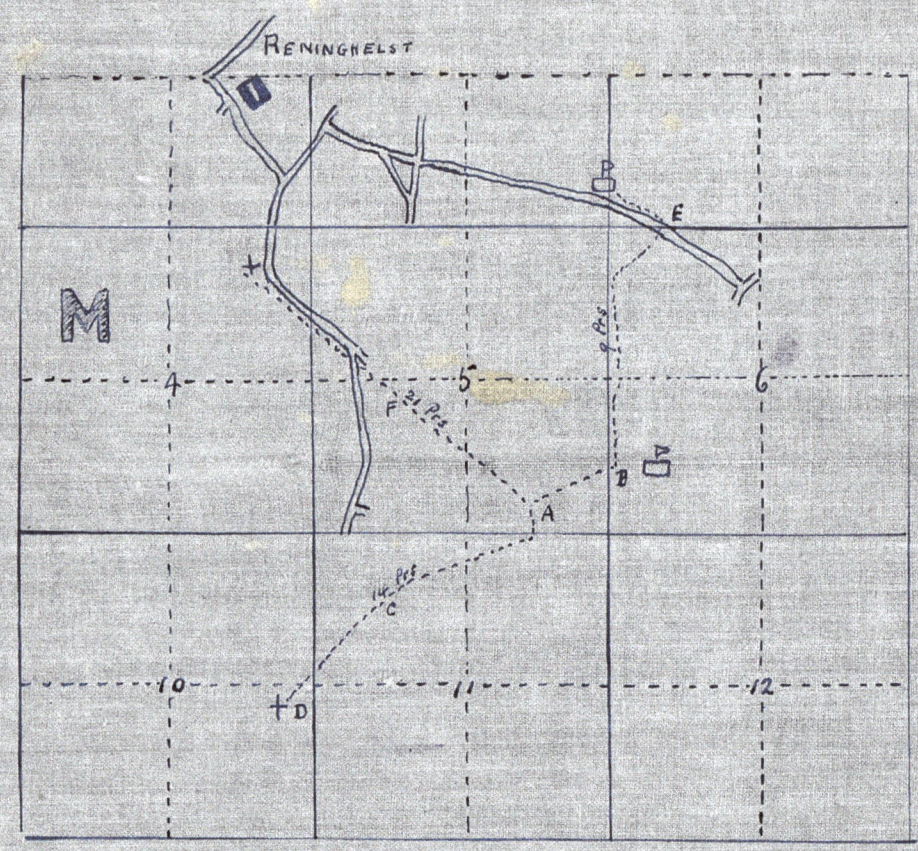

LEGEND
⌂ Brigade Hq.
------ Route of Bury.

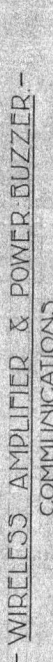

Appendix C.

– WIRELESS AMPLIFIER & POWER BUZZER –
COMMUNICATIONS.

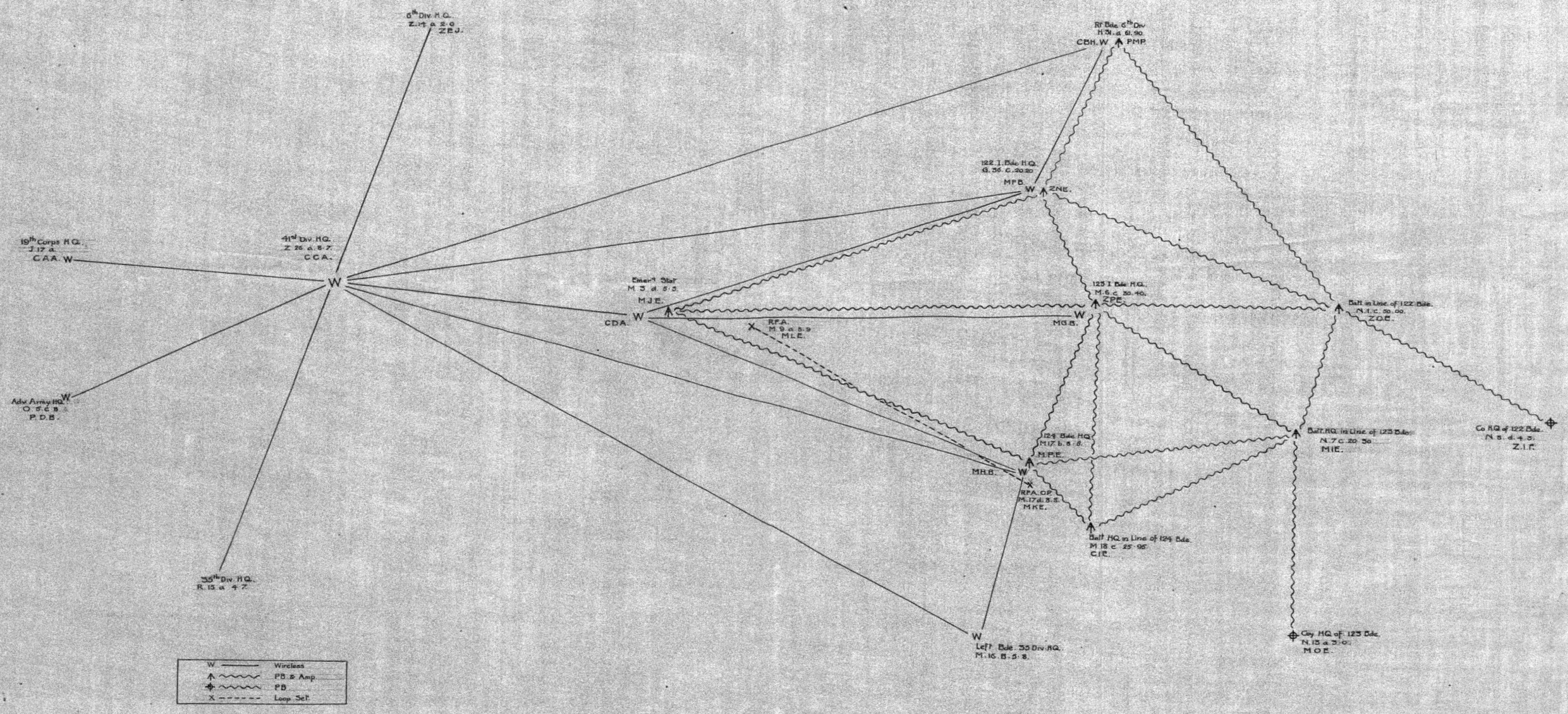

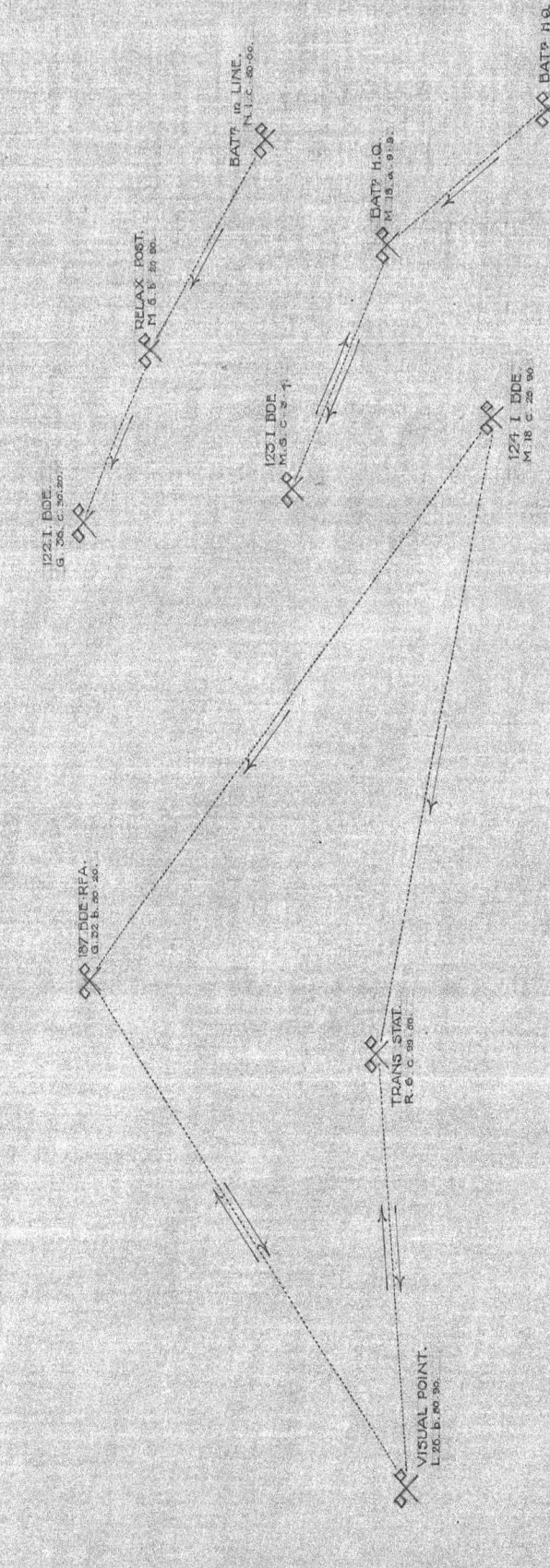

Appendix E.

ROUTE DIAGRAM
41ST DIVISIONAL SIGNAL COY.

Appendix. E.

Appendix H

WIRELESS-POWER-BUZZER & AMPLIFIER
— COMMUNICATIONS —

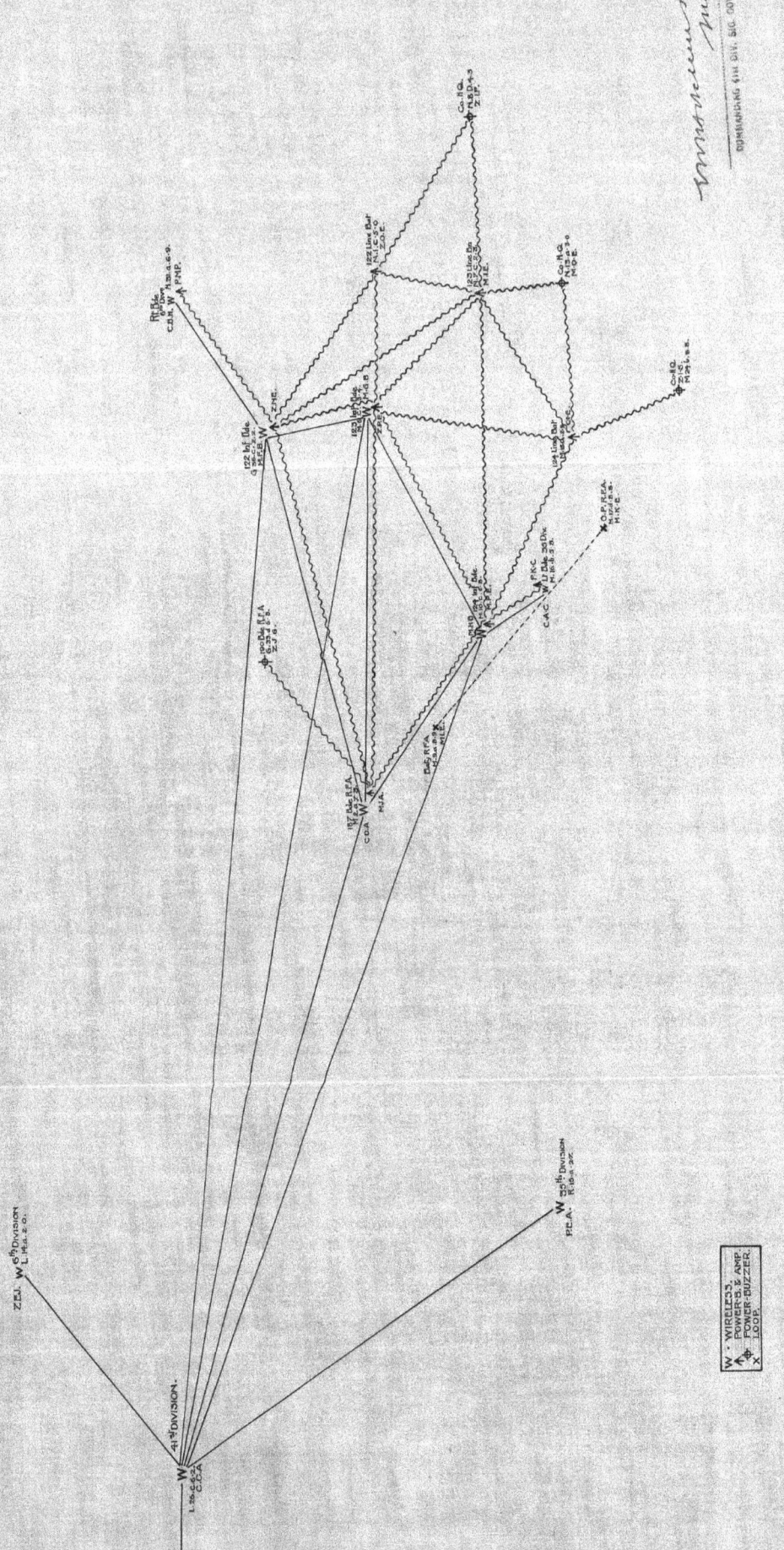

Appendix G.

VISUAL
— COMMUNICATIONS —
41ST DIVISIONAL SIGNAL COY.

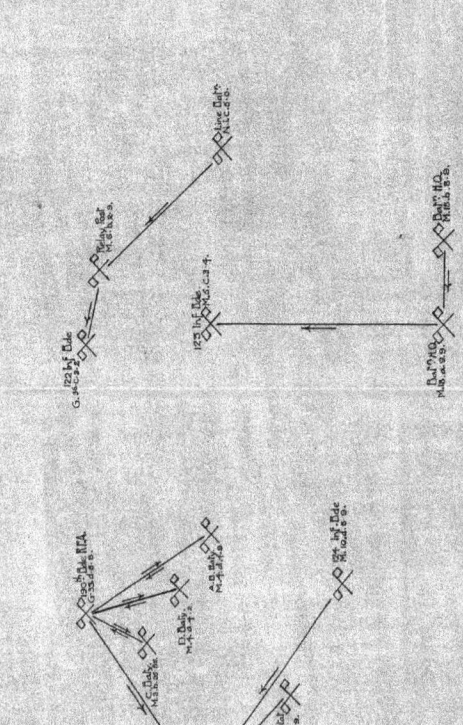

WAR DIARY
INTELLIGENCE SUMMARY
(Erase heading not required.)

Army Form C. 2118.

41 D Signals Vol 28

Place	Date	Hour	Summary of Events and Information	Remarks and references to Appendices
HUT CAMP K 24 C 2.3	1/8/18		A working party of 40 Infantry were finished marking the Divisional Buried Cable Route in daylight.	
	2/8/18		Instructions were received to move the Divisional Signal School from RUBROUCK. This matter is being pushed, and results are awaited.	
	3/8/18		The Signal Company entered teams in the 2nd Army Horse Show at BAVINCHOVE. The turn outs were very good but failed to get a prize.	
	4/8/18		About 8 am the enemy heavily shelled the area just South of RENINGHELST with shells up to a calibre of 8" and at 8.30 am the buried Cable Route was cut in two areas in two places. It so happens A. with 4 linemen were working in the shell holes at 10 am, the shelling still being very heavy. The Cornes lines were through by 10.15 am and the whole of the Buried Cable Route was restored by 2.10 pm. This meant the making of 168 holes under very difficult conditions and was a very creditable performance on the part of B.C. Oliver Davies and the linemen concerned.	
	5/8/18		It was necessary this day to allow Infantry labour to fill in the shell holes on, or about, the buried cable route which was made during the enemy's shelling on the 4th inst.	

WAR DIARY
INTELLIGENCE SUMMARY
(Erase heading not required.)

Army Form C. 2118.

Place	Date	Hour	Summary of Events and Information	Remarks and references to Appendices
HUT CAMP R24 C.2.3.	6/7/18		The Buried Cable route put down by the French between to Dieppe Belfort to group Tircule and requires up to 450' of earth. This makes telephone conversation poor. The manus Battle routes are being changed into 10 pair staked cable route from L.L. to C.H., thence formed in the Army to F.L. See diag & attd Appendix A	Appendix A.
	7/7/18		Communications for a trench operation on the front of 122 Infy Bde were worked out by O/C Signals and the Brigade Signalling Officer vide Appendix A att'd	Appendix A
			The Hostile shelling of the Rest Area has increased of recent date and takes the form of violent shell storms, including shells up to 8" calibre which are often near the buried cable route. It is not considered that the enemy are actually shooting at the buried route, but a great deal of work is necessitated by filling in the shell holes on or near to the buried route. For this purpose regular patrols have been instituted who will patrol the beng at fixed periods to fill in shell holes and to report all O.K. or otherwise to Signal Co. at H.Q. via the main Dist forward test point at A.A. Box.	

WAR DIARY
INTELLIGENCE SUMMARY.
(Erase heading not required.)

Army Form C. 2118.

	Date	Hour	Summary of Events and Information	Remarks and references to Appendices
HUT CAMP K24 C 2 3	8/8/18		A quiet day on the lines to day. The overground route to CH is now through and we are awaiting for the Corps to complete the FL Buzz before joining up and changing the receiver. Trouble with Corps lines which caused some anxiety as a minor operation was to take place at midnight. By this time however the working of all battle lines was restored. The attack was to be made on a battalion front of the left Brigade with objectives about 500 yds in advance of the starting line. The battalion was the 15th Hants. about seventy keen withdrawn for special training as storm troops and many of communication had been carefully practised over similar ground. Phone communication was by spiral cable on the following chain. Front line post (N14.c.5.10) to Advance Battalion (N7.b.9.5) to Battalion Report Centre N14 a 7.6 to Brigade Head quarters (G.3.b.c.2.1) The line between the Front line H/Q and the Advance bn H/Q went down from about 12.5 am till 12.20 am after being repaired but happen to lasted throughout the night. The line from advance Bn H/Qrs to Bn Report Centre was dis. from overnight till nearly 1 am owing to enemy barrage	
	9/8/18			

Army Form C. 2118.

WAR DIARY
or
INTELLIGENCE SUMMARY.
(Erase heading not required.)

Place	Date	Hour	Summary of Events and Information	Remarks and references to Appendices
HUT CAMP R24C2.3	8/8/18		Communication was established with the front line H/Q wire with the Bde O.P. who shared the same line by about 1 am after much commune- was uninterrupted all other lines held throughout the operations. The aeroplanes attacked Hqrs N.C4570 was jammed from about 12.45 am until 1 am by Boche wireless but otherwise worked well. Wireless was not possible owing to front country as a hedge in position but were not required. Rocket troughs were in position but were not required. It was not necessary to use pigeons. The attack went much as all operations precedent. The commanding officer Lt Col E.N.F. Hitchins went on leave, the command of the Battalion being taken over by Capt W.W. Scott-Thorough RE. the reserves in ammunition still trouble our Corps has not nected. We received the mutation of the Lt. Ch. pole cable route. It has been experienced that 75.6 miles of 7 pain have absorbed. Tried so to try to obtain good speech. The resistance of this length is great and though lines been taken up earth the speech is very faint from over such a distance.	
	9/8/18			

Army Form C. 2118.

WAR DIARY
or
INTELLIGENCE SUMMARY.

(Erase heading not required.)

Instructions regarding War Diaries and Intelligence Summaries are contained in F.S. Regs., Part II. and the Staff Manual respectively. Title pages will be prepared in manuscript.

Place	Date	Hour	Summary of Events and Information	Remarks and references to Appendices
HUT CAMP K2 c.2.3.	9/8 cont		Wire buried cable put therefore to heavy transference further found that. Newspapers the Bury Reg'ts in to about 4 to 5 Stwhs. It made my recent Brock Copper-conductors to this point (O.H.) that the checking will be improved.	
	10/8		The enemy's snipers attacked on the new front gained by the 15th Bn Scouts Reg'ts. He was driven off. It was a misty morning and pigeons were free with messages and several hours late. The message, which would for authority before therefore in use.	
	11/8		K-64 went to reconnoitred and a great engagement on which rests. Working party out on LL-PS points. Staking, repairing and reconnoitring some history of importance to report.	
	12/8 13/8		LL-PS points continued. Quiet day.	
	13/14/8 15/16		Listing to report on three days except that working parties were out in the broken back areas. Tidying up & carrying on &c.	

Army Form C. 2118.

WAR DIARY
INTELLIGENCE SUMMARY
(Erase heading not required.)

Place	Date	Hour	Summary of Events and Information	Remarks and references to Appendices
HUT CAMP K24 C 2.3	17/18		The 41st Divl Signal School was moved from RUBROUCK to CRANHIL Sheet 27 N.W. H16 d2.0. The 66th Divl Arty relieved the 41st Divl Arty in the line on the 17/18 - 18/19 the latter going to ST LAURENT	
	18/8/18		On this night a new buried cable was begun from LA CLYTTE to Headquarters of 122 Infy Bde G 36 c.1.2. The working party was shelled in LA CLYTTE and four men were killed. About 300 yds of the line were laid down.	
	19/8/18		On this night the burying party at LA CLYTTE were again progressing. The night was quieter. Without what completed	
	20/8/18		The burying party was cancelled on this night owing to the operations in the 30th Division on our left	
	21/8/18		The working party which was sent up was detailed to complete what had been left undone occurred at about 9.30 p.m.; at about 10.45 p.m. the enemy S.O.S. went up and a barrage came down upon the men who protected. They were again called that were unable to work owing to heavy shelling all night.	

Army Form C. 2118.

WAR DIARY
or
INTELLIGENCE SUMMARY.
(Erase heading not required.)

Place	Date	Hour	Summary of Events and Information	Remarks and references to Appendices
HUT CAMP No. 2 & 3	22/5/18		Decided to give the LA CLYTTE bury a rest. Orders were issued to begin the lateral from S.C. to the left along the SCHERPENBERG – LA CLYTTE road. Arrangements were made for two shifts of 100 men each to work from 6 a.m. till noon, and from 2 p.m. until 8 p.m. See copy of orders and mah attached.	Appendix B.
	23/5/18		Work on the SCHERPENBERG – LA CLYTTE bury commenced and satisfactory progress was made.	
	24/5/18		All points in the buried cable under the control of this Divisional Signal Co. were this day carefully marked with markers.	
	25/5/18		Work on the lateral bury continued.	
	26/5/18		The system of holding the Brit front is being changed tonight at 12 midnight. There will be two Bdes in the line and one in Reserve. Communications were adjusted in accordance with the new conditions. Orders were received late in night for the relief of the 41st Div. in the line by the 34th Div.	

Army Form C. 2118.

WAR DIARY
OF
INTELLIGENCE SUMMARY.
(Erase heading not required.)

Instructions regarding War Diaries and Intelligence Summaries are contained in F. S. Regs., Part II. and the Staff Manual respectively. Title pages will be prepared in manuscript.

Place	Date	Hour	Summary of Events and Information	Remarks and references to Appendices
HUT CAMP K24 c 2 3	27/8.		O/C Sigs 41 Div conducted O/C Signals 34 Div round the communications of the Forward Div Area.	
	28/8.		O/C Sigs 34 Div was conducted round (communications of Div Back Areas. Horse Transport left for WIZERNES under 2nd Lt Fenston starting at 12 noon and staying at RENISCURE	
	29/8		O/C Signals 34 Div took over control of Communications in the Div Area at Noon, everything being in working order. The Signal Coy less Horse Transport personnel left for WIZERNES by rail & Motor Lorry in accordance with Appendix C attached	Appendix C
WIZERNES	30/8		Company settled into Billets at WIZERNES. Schemes for training programme were drawn up	
	31/8		Owing to the enemy withdrawal on the 2nd Army front Warning orders were received to take over the DICKEBUSCH Sector from the 27th American Div at 10 a.m. on the 3rd of Sept.	

mmmmmm
Major.
Duke of Wellington Regt.
O/C Signals 41 Div.

Army Form C. 2118.

WAR DIARY
— of —
INTELLIGENCE SUMMARY.
(Erase heading not required.)

Instructions regarding War Diaries and Intelligence Summaries are contained in F. S. Regs., Part II. and the Staff Manual respectively. Title pages will be prepared in manuscript.

Place	Date	Hour	Summary of Events and Information	Remarks and references to Appendices
HUT CAMP K24 C 2. 3.	1/7/18		2/Lt Prentis S.F arrived from Base Signal Depot.	
	2/7/18		1.O.R evacuated to 2nd Can. C.C.S.	
	5/7/18		2/Lt Prentis S.F evacuated to 64th C.C.S.	
	9/7/18		2/Lieut Pettence left the Coy for duty at S.S.T.C. Bedford 1.O.R evacuated to 2 Can. C.C.S	
	12/7/18		1.O.R awarded Bar to M.M.	
	13/7/18		1.O.R slightly wounded. Remaining at Duty	
	14/7/18		2.O.Rs Wounded and admitted to Hospl.	
	16/7/18		1.O.R. joined from Base Signal Depot	
	18/7/18		1.O.R. Wounded & admitted to Hospl.	
	23/7/18		1.O.R joined from Base Signal Depot 1.O.R evacuated to C.C.S	
	24/7/18		1.O.R evacuated to C.C.S. 1.O.R departed for England	
	26/7/18		1.O.R joined from Base Signal Depot	
	27/7/18		2.O.Rs evacuated to C.C.S	
	28/7/18		1 R.S.M, 1 Sgt. R.E. joined from 2nd Army	
	29/7/18		1.O.R left for England	
	30/7/18		2 O.Rs joined from Base Signal Depot 1 Sgt/Inch left the Coy to join the 3rd S/d Sig Coy Lt Brennan act. as Supernumerary was posted to the Coy	

M.P.M
Duke of Wellington Regt
O/c Signals 41 Division

SECRET.

Appendix. A

PROPOSED COMMUNICATIONS

FOR 122nd INFANTRY BRIGADE OPERATION ORDER No. 209.

Ref. Map Sheet 28 S.W. KEMMEL 1/10000

1. **TELEPHONE.**
    A Line will be run from Advanced Battalion Headquarters, N.7.b.9.5, to Battalion Forward Report Centre which will be established in dug-outs near CLYDESDALE FARM about N.14.a.7.6.

2. **POWER BUZZER & AMPLIFIER.**
    A Power Buzzer will be taken by Battalion Forward Party who will instal same at the Forward Report Centre N.14.a.7.6, and work to Power Buzzer and Amplifier at Advanced Battalion Headquarters N.7.b.9.5.   Advanced Battalion Headquarters will work direct to Power Buzzer and Amplifier at Brigade. The Power Buzzer and Amplifier Station at the Front Line Headquarters N.1.c.45.10 will remain silent unless they hear Brigade Station are unable to get the Signals.

3. **VISUAL.**
    Battalion Forward Party will arrange visual from the Forward Report Centre to Advanced Battalion Headquarters via a transmitting station.

4. **PIGEONS.**
    4 at Advanced Battalion Headquarters, 4 at Battalion Forward Report Centre and 2 each with two Companies of attacking troops. (Total 12 Pigeons.)

5. **MESSAGE ROCKETS.**
    From MILLEKRUISSE, N.2.c.70.15, to Front Line Battalion Headquarters, N.1.c.45.10, and from Advanced Battalion Headquarters, N.7.b.9.5, to the Support Battalion Headquarters M.6.d.4.6. *also from Front Line Hqrs to Brigade*

6. **RUNNERS.**
    Brigade will establish Relay Post at Front Line Battalion Headquarters N.1.c.45.10.   Messages will be sent by runner from Forward Report Centre to Advanced Battalion Headquarters thence to Front Line Battalion Headquarters on to Brigade. The Front Line Battalion will be responsible for messages going forward from Brigade Relay Post to Advanced Battalion Headquarters.

DIARY.

Appendix. B.

Scherpenberg – La Clytte Lateral Bury

Arrangements

Route and Weight of Cables. The route selected is as per tracing attached and the figures show the number of pairs required.

Dump. The forward dump from which cable will be drawn is a shell hole where the De Seu Cabaret track joins the SCHERPENBERG – La Clytte road at about M17 b 95.80.

Labour. Labour has been arranged as follows

Shift "A" 100 strong with 100 shovels and 50 picks will report to rendezvous daily at 6 a.m. (M17 b 95.80)

Shift "B" 100 strong with 100 shovels and 50 picks will report to same rendezvous at 2 p.m. daily

Specification. The trench is to be dug six feet deep, the required number of pairs laid and filled in complete by each shift.

Tasks. Each man will be required to dig two yards and fill in. 200 yds per shift per day is therefore expected.

Laying the Cable. The Divisional linemen at S.C. test point (Sprs Cawley and Masters) will lay out the cable with each shift.

Jointing. The jointing of the cable will be done under Divisional arrangements. Care must be taken to have about 2 yds of open trench at each joint and a sufficient quantity of slack

Officers Duty Roster

Lt. Dyke	'A'	Shift	23rd inst	6. am
Lt. Thompson	'B'	"	-do-	2. pm
Lt. Harvey	'A'	"	24 inst	6. am
Lt. Lush	'B'	"	do	2. pm

Officers will be at the rendezvous at times detailed for each shift and take charge of the work. Each will hand over any particulars or peculiarities necessary to the officer doing duty on the shift succeeding his own.

After the 24th inst. a readjustment of rendezvous and cable dump may be necessary.

Details of this will be given in good time.

Routes will be personally re-considered beforehand.

Addressed to
 O.C. Signals 122 Infy Bde
 " " 123 "
 " " 124 "
 " No 5 Sect. M.G.C.

Repeated.
 41. Div. G.
 B.M. 122. Bde *
 " 123 " *
 " 124 " *
 A.D. Signals Corps

} For information
* (without maps)

Acknowledge

     [signature]
     Capt.
    O.C. 4th Div. Sig. Co RE

FF 625   Appendix "C"

Secret   41st Divl Signal Co RE
          Order No 41

1) The 41st Divl Signal Co less one Cable Detachment and 1 MT which later will move to Wisques by rail and road will commence 28 inst.

2) All horse transport and riding horses will march under command of Lt FENELON at 2 pm on 29.5.18
Starting point road junction R.3.b.1.3
Time of start 2 pm
Destination RENESCURE
Route QUAET MAFLE — OXELAERE — HAVINGHOVE — LE NIEPPE — will proceed to follow Company of MGB

29-5-18 Starting point RENESCURE
Time 8 am to M HERNES
Rte E HERNES

3) L. BRENNAN will arrange for the dispatch of stores to direct to M. HERNES

GF 625

1. The remaining personnel of the Coy will move on the 30th inst, by road, and rail to WIZERNES under instructions to be issued later.

2. Lt Sylvester will arrange for the move of the office relief and stores.

3. O/C Wireless will arrange for the transport of wireless personnel & stores on relief.

Acknowledge.

Copies to No 1   O/C Signals
                2   Lt Sylvester
                3   Lt Brennan
                4   Lt Fenelon
                5   Lt Dawson
                6   C.M.S.
                7   Diary
                8   File

                                    W. Hutchins
27/8/18.   Major
                              O/C Signals 4th Divn

WAR DIARY
INTELLIGENCE SUMMARY
(Erase heading not required)

Army Form C. 2118.

41 D Signals

Place	Date	Hour	Summary of Events and Information	Remarks and references to Appendices
WIZERNES	1/7/18		O.C. Signals visited 27th American Division and made preliminary arrangements for taking over the line on the 3rd inst.	
	2/7/18		L'Sylvester with Office relief and linesmen proceeded to DOUGLAS CAMP H/Q of 27th American Division with a view to taking over the following day. Horse Transport started to move. It was this day a reconnaissance with 41 Div Signal Co. Orders No. 42. See Appendix A attached	Appx A
DOUGLAS CAMP L.14.a.2.0	3/7/18		Relief of the American Div Signals completed at 10 am. Communications are working all right but it is difficult to find out exactly what we have and how lines run as the American reports are not up to date and their Signal Officers do not appear very well informed as to the situation.	
	4/7/18		In conjunction with troops on our right we made a reconnaissance in force towards the WYTSCHAETE RIDGE. Communications naturally owing to the shortness of time had not been worked out in a very thorough manner but they worked satisfactorily.	
	5/7/18		O.C. Signals reconnoitred the old buried cable from HALLEBAST CORNER towards WERSTRAAT with a view to restoring it. It was laced with some difficulty as far as J.T.1304 at N.4.d.1.5 and 2 sappers with a working party	

WAR DIARY
INTELLIGENCE SUMMARY

Army Form C. 2118.

Place	Date	Hour	Summary of Events and Information	Remarks and references to Appendices
DOUGLAS CAMP L.14.a.2.0	5/9/18		of 4 Infantry men started work on it	
	6/9/18		Amplifier and P/B communications were arranged in accordance with Appendix B attached	Appdx. B
	7/9/18		No 4 Sect at WALKERS FARM were badly gassed and one officer and 13 O.Rs were evacuated. The gassing resumed owing to the hut occupied by the Bns Guard receiving a direct hit by a 5.9in Yellow Cross gas shell. The occupants attached with the Bns signal section into the Signal office for over twenty four hours, the men in the office.	
	8/9/18		Communications were completed for the 2nd Front being held by one Brigade	
	9/9/18		Nothing to report. Restoration work is being continued successfully on the old HALLEBAST CORNER Buzy	
	10/9/18		A visual system of Communications between Brigades and Battns is now established and working in accordance with Appendix C attached.	Appdx. C

Army Form C. 2118.

WAR DIARY
or
INTELLIGENCE SUMMARY.
(Erase heading not required.)

Instructions regarding War Diaries and Intelligence Summaries are contained in F. S. Regs., Part II. and the Staff Manual respectively. Title pages will be prepared in manuscript.

Place	Date	Hour	Summary of Events and Information	Remarks and references to Appendices
Douglas CAMP L144.2.c.	11 Sept 1915		20 out of 21 hrs have been put through on the old HALLEBAST CORNER-VIERSTRAAT Bury, as far as J.T. Box and some have been taken onto use this day. It is remarkable the way the buried cable has withstood the Heavy Artillery fire and the enemy had not destroyed the Test Boxes when they were in his possession.	
	12 "		Efforts are being made to extend the old buried route beyond J.T. Box but the chances of success appear poor.	
	13 "		O/C Signals visited all Battys in the Div Area and inspected their Communications which are working satisfactorily.	
	14 "		Plans were made for starting work on a new buried cable system to extend the old buried cable to the back from HALLEBAST CORNER toward HAGUE FARM. 300 men will start work on this on the 16th inst.	
	15 "		Signalling Instructions for Dusk Defence Scheme were prepared and handed to the General Staff. Copies attached vide Appendix "D"	Appendix D
	16 "		The new buried route of 21 pairs now started from HALLEBAST CORNER towards HAGUE FARM to connect the buried old route which terminates at Pt.2 to the new buried route which terminates at H.F.	
	17 "		A separate Test Box at HALLEBAST CORNER at the Junction of the new route old routes	

WAR DIARY
INTELLIGENCE SUMMARY
(Erase heading not required.)

Army Form C. 2118.

Place	Date	Hour	Summary of Events and Information	Remarks and references to Appendices
DOUGLAS CAMP L.14.a.2.0	Sept 17		Routes mentioned above started this day. The 6th course at the Divl Cyclist School finished and the 7th course assembled.	
	18		Nothing to report.	
	19		The new bury from HALLEBAST CROSS ROADS is now finished to about H.32.a.1.3. Others have decided not to bury cable beyond this point which is behind the Battery area, but to constitute this route with attached cables.	
	20		Conferences and reconnaissances for projected operations. 122 Inf.y Bde H/Q moved from HAGUE FARM to ZEVECOTEN. The Division is ready in support with one brigade out training at LICAUSSE.	
	21		Further Conferences and reconnaissances for the left (?) operations.	
	22, 23		Operation Instructions No.43 completed and issued on 23rd inst. Appendix E attached	App/14 E
	24, 25, 26		Nothing to report.	
	27		Suspens moved to their Stations in accordance with Signal Instructions No 43. Div H/Q moved from Douglas Camp to be in force at 4 p.m. All Lines and Wireless were through at 10 p.m.	

Army Form C. 2118.

WAR DIARY
or
INTELLIGENCE SUMMARY.
(Erase heading not required.)

Place	Date 1918	Hour	Summary of Events and Information	Remarks and references to Appendices
MERSEY FARM	28 Sep.		The attack started at 5.30 a.m. 124 Bde moved up to SWAN CHATEAU and got into Communication at 7.30 a.m. The 123 Bde did not move according to plan but turned out both BRANDHOEK and SWAN CHATEAU H/Q with the result that they were not in Communication for a space of 6 hours. At 9.30 a.m. 124 J Bde moved to LARCH WOOD. Wireless communication was established at once and Wire Communication about 2 hours later. 123 Infy Bde H/Q moved to VERBRANDEN MOLEN was repaired with them via 124 J Bde H/Q. 122 Infy Bde moved to SWAN CHATEAU about 5pm. 124 J Bde H/Q moved to Sheet 28 P.I.C.2.4. It was impossible to get a cable wagon to them that night owing to there being at the other side of the water are into no wagons through. Wireless Communication was established with them during the night. 124 Inf Bde at P.I.C.2.4. obtained wire communication at about 10 am after great difficulties owing to the state of roads and congestion of traffic.	
	29 "	5 pm	At 5 pm Divl H/Q moved to LANKHOF FARM Sheet 28 H.26.c.c.0. and the Divl Signal forward Station was established at P.I.C.2.4 near the H/Q of the 124 J Bde. 123 Infy Bde moved up to KORTEWILDE and a line was run to them from the Divl Forward Exchange. 122 J Bde moved to the vicinity of TENBRIELEN and a line was also laid to them from the Divl Fd. Statn.	
LANKHOF FARM			These lines were maintained with great difficulty owing to a certain	

Army Form C. 2118.

WAR DIARY
~~or~~ INTELLIGENCE SUMMARY.
(Erase heading not required.)

Place	Date 1918	Hour	Summary of Events and Information	Remarks and references to Appendices
LANKHOF FARM	Sept 29		to a certain extent to hostile shell fire but chiefly to the state of the roads and congestion of traffic.	
	30		Two more lines were run out between Div. H/S. LANKHOF FARM and the Divl. Attd Station. This enormously improved line communication.	

P.W.Kearey. Major R.E.
O.C. Signals 41 Divn

Army Form C. 2118.

WAR DIARY
or
INTELLIGENCE SUMMARY.
(Erase heading not required.)

Instructions regarding War Diaries and Intelligence Summaries are contained in F. S. Regs., Part II. and the Staff Manual respectively. Title pages will be prepared in manuscript.

Place	Date	Hour	Summary of Events and Information	Remarks and references to Appendices
	1918 Sept 4		One OR arrived from Base Signal Depot	
	7		Lt Hy Thompson 2 ORs 2 ats gunshot left for 6.4 Div Signal Co. hurriedly	
			1 Offr (Lt. J. Crowther 27th May attd Signal Co.) + 13 ORs joined	
	8		One OR evacuated	
	9		Lt F.R. Aherd Wills Rey arrived from 2 3rd Div Signal Co. 1 OR arrived with him 1 OR evacuated	
	10		1 OR evacuated	
	12		5 ORs arrived from Base Signal Depot. 1 OR evacuated to C.C.S.	
			Capt. W.W. Scott moved (1 Strike) to Strength of B.E.F.	
	16		Major H.H. Lacey WE H'company	
	17		1 OR evacuated on a recently accident	
	20		1 OR arrived from Base Signal Depot	
	21		1 OR evacuated	
	25		1 OR reported from Hosp. 1 OR attd evacuated to CCS	
	26		2 ORs evacuated	
	27		1 OR do	
	29		1 OR wounded to Field	
	30		1 OR wounded accidentally	

F.H. Lacey. Major WE
O.C. Signal to A1 Divn

FF(a) Copy No 6   Appendix. A.

21st Divisional Signal Co. R.E. Order No 42

(1) The Horse Transport of the Coy will move to-morrow under Lt Fenelon
   Starting Pt. Fork road WIZERNES — ST OMER
                immediately West of ARQUES.
   Time   2.30 pm
   Destination ZEGGERSCAPPEL
   Route   ARQUES NIEURLET ZUDPEENE

   The Signal Coy will follow the CRE HT[?] in order of Lading.

(2) The march will be continued on the morning of the 3rd inst.

(3) Final Destination of transport will be notified later.

(4) Acknowledge

   Copy No 1 O.C.
        2   2/Lt Fenelon
        3   Lt Sylvester
        4   Lt Brennan   [signature]
        5   CRMS   Major
        6   Diary   O/C Signals 21st Div"

Appendix B.

WIRELESS, P.B. & AMPLIFIER COMMUNICATIONS
71st DIVISION.

Appendix. C.

VISUAL COMMUNICATIONS.
41ST DIVISION.

Appendix. D

Instruction No.

Signalling Arrangements in the 41st Divl Area.

1. Division to the Brigade in the line and Brigade in Support.

   (a) Telegraphic & Telephonic Communications are obtained by means of Buried Cable Routes and air Lines. All lines within the shelled area are buried cable, and there are two alternate routes. These communications therefore can be considered safe.

   (b) Wireless. The Brigade in the line and Bde in support are in direct communication with the Wilson Directing Set at Divl H/Q.

   (c) Motor Cyclist Despatch Riders can ride direct to Brigade H/Qs from Division.

2. Lateral Communications.

   (a) Divisional H/Q is in communication with the Divisions on the Rt & Lt by safe Telegraph and Telephone Routes and also by Wireless.

   (b) The Brigade in the line is in Lateral Communication with the Brigades on the Rt & Left by Buried Cable Routes & by wireless.

3. Communications Forward of Brigades.

   (a) The Bde in the line is in Telegraphic & Telephonic Communication with the two front line & Rt Support Battalions by ground lines to Hallebast to N4D15, thence on a restored old buried Route, thence overground to the Battn H/Q.

   A new buried cable route is in course of construction from Hallebast Corner towards HAGUE ~~Hag~~ Farm.

   To the Support Battn in H.28.d.4.1 communication is obtained by Buried Cable to Walker Farm H.27.b.6.6 ~~thence overground~~ to Q Box in H.27.d.

3. cont.

thence by a restored Old Buried Route to F.Q Box in H.28.d.9.1, thence overground to Battⁿ.

(b) P/B and Amplifier.

The two front line Battⁿˢ are in Common by P/B to the Brigade in accordance with Appendix A attached.

(c) Visual.

The Brigade in the line is in Communication with the Right Front line Battⁿ & the Left Support Battalion as shown in Appendix B attached.

4. Communications in Advance of Battⁿ H/Q.

(a) The two Front line Battⁿˢ are in communication with their Companies by overground lines.

(b) By P/B vide Appendix A.

(c) By means of Pigeons

(d) " " of Messenger Dogs.

(e) " " of Rockets.

5. A scheme of Artillery Communications will be forwarded later.

D.N. Hitchens.
Major
Duke of Wellington's Regt.

14 9/18

Signalling Arrangements in the 41st Divl. Area.

Artillery Communications.

(1) To Right Group (187 Bde.)
1 Ringing Line. Buried to Inf. Bde. H/Q, airline to Right Group.
1 Buzzer Line as above.

To Left Group (190 Bde.)
2 Ringing lines. Buried to B.T. airline to W.F. Buried to Left Group

C.W. Wireless is now working from D.A. H/Q to Rt. Group.

(2) 2 Ringing Lines from R.A. H.Qrs to 41 Divl. Exchange.
1 Line to Divl. Exchange on Right.
1 Line to R.A. do of Divn on Left.
1 Line to a heavy Artillery Bde.
1 Line to Corps Hennes.

Rt. Group has an airline to the Inf. Bde. it covers.
Two Batteries of the Right Group have one common line to the Right Battalion in the line.
Left Group has an airline to the Infantry Bde in the line, also a lateral line to Right Group & to the Group on their left.

3. Right Group has 2 lines to B. battery's main position one of which is buried from F.C.2. They have also a direct line to A. C. & D. batteries each.
B Battery has a lateral to each of the other Batteries.
Left Group:
1 Line to each of B. C. & D. batteries

3. cont'd

Laterals from
A to B.   B to C.
B main to B. forward with D to B forward Sect.

4. Right Group. Two OPs in line

A. OP   1 airline to B Battery
         1 airline to J.T., bussed to F.C. 2 airline
         to C. Batty.

B. OP   1 airline to D battery
         1   "   to B battery.

Route Diagram attached.

Signalling Arrangements in the 41st Divisional Area.

Machine Gun Communications.

Telephone.

Between the Battalion Headquarters and the Forward Units all communications are through the Divisional System, either to Advanced Divisional Exchange or the Infantry Brigades in Line.

The Support and Reserve Companies are connected to the Advanced Divisional Exchange, while the Forward Companies are connected to the Infantry Brigade Exchanges respectively.

One Section of each Forward Company is connected to an Advanced Infantry Battalion Exchange. Fullerphones are working on these lines.

The Right Company has a direct line to a rear Section. This is the Machine Gun Section Report Centre and is central to all Sections in the Right Front area.

A Section Report Centre is being established at Wiltshire Farm for use of the Left Company Sections.

Lateral.

Forward Companies have communication by wire via Infantry Brigade Exchanges.

Runners

A regular service, twice daily, is established between Battalion Headquarters, Machine Gun Report Centre ie adv. B'att'n and Companies. Company Runners to Forward Sections

Runners.
(cont'd)
　　under Company arrangements.

Pigeons.
　　Two birds are delivered daily at Infantry Brigade Headquarters for use of the Right Company.

Diagram of Communications attached.

Appendix E
Copy No. 18

Very Secret

Signal Instructions No 43

(1) On ~~the night of the 24th~~ /25th Sept Div H/Q will be at G 36 c 2·2 *a date to be notified later*

124 I. Bde H/Q will be at in Square G 18 b.
123   "   "   at Dominion Farm G 24 a 2·5
122   "   "   at Hoograf Camp G 26·c

All connected by buried cables.

(2). A Div. Forward Signal Station and Exchange will be established at Q Box H 27 d 8·6 which will be in buried cable and Visual Signalling Communication with Div. H/Q.

Three Cable Wagons with Detachments (1 for the use of the RA) will be assembled in the vicinity of Q Box in the early morning of ~~the 25 Sept.~~ ZERO DAY

One Cable Wagon with Detachment complete will be kept in Reserve at DHQ.

3. Wireless Stations all under supervision of Lt Stanworth will be attached as follows

    2 Stations to 124 Infy Bde.
    1   "   123   "
    1   "   122   "

C.W. Sets will be at the disposal of the RA.
A Wilson directing set will be at DHQ

At 7 am ~~on 25.9.17~~ on ZERO DAY one of the Wireless Stations allotted to 124 Inf Bde will be erected at the 2nd H/Q of the 124 Inf Bde which will be in the vicinity of Swan Chateau: E 19·c (Exact position will be notified later)

The 2nd Trench Set with the 124 Infy Bde will be in the vicinity and will be used for stepping up purposes as the Bde advances.

The Trench Sets of the 122 + 123 Infy Bdes will move with the Bde H/Q but will not be brought into action unless other means of Communication have failed

(4) A Cable Wagon under the orders of Lt Sylvester will connect the 2nd H/Q of the 124 Infy Bde to the buried cable at Q box and will remain in the vicinity of the 124 Infy Bde H/Q and move with them as far as the situation permits.

123 & 122 Infy Bdes will occupy in turn the H/Q vacated by the 124 Infy Bde and will Tee on to the Divl. overground line which will be indicated to them by a Divl Lineman, and thus obtain wire communication to Divn.

(5) The 190 Bde R.F.A will be connected by a Cable wagon line to the Exchange at Q Box when they come under 41st Divl control and take up their position in the vicinity of Middlesex Road, probably somewhere in square I 27.

O.C. Signals 41 D Arty will be responsible for the laying and maintaining of this line with a Cable Wagon and Detachment at his disposal.

This Cable wagon will remain in the vicinity of the 190 Bde R.F.A H/Q and will follow up any further moves as far as circumstances permit.

The 187 Bde R.F.A and a Bde of the 14th Divl Arty will communicate to Divl. H/Q via the 190 Bde H/Q as soon as possible after they take up their Forward positions and come under the command of the G.O.C. 41 Divn.

(6) Brigade Forward Parties besides their usual personnel and Equipment will be supplemented from H/Q Divl Signal Co as follows:—

(6) cont'd.

Each with
1 Amplifier / personnel of 3 O.Rs.
2 P/Bs for inter-Bde communication.
4 men from the Divl. Amplifier Section as
a carrying party for Wireless Stores.

They will also receive an issue of Pigeons
and Message Carrying Rockets as follows:—

	Pigeons	Message Carrying Rockets
124 Infy Bde	20	4 Boxes. *
123 "	10	3 "
122 "	10	3 "

*(These Boxes contain 8 Rockets complete with Stand in each Box)

Two Boxes of Message Carrying Rockets will be
at the Disposal of O.C. Sigs. 41 Divl. Arty.

(7) The Divl. O.O. will be supplied with 12
Pigeons.

He will also run a line from his Battle
H/Q to the Exchange at Q Box which will put
him in telephone communication with D.H.Q.

(8) A Forward Signal Dump containing cable,
a limited number of D⁂ Telephones and
Message Carrying Rockets will be established
at Q Box on the night before Zero Day.

Issues will be made from this Dump on
an officer's signature after Zero hour.

(9) Two Motor Cyclists will be on Duty at Q Box
and 1 extra Motor Cyclist will be attached to H/Q
of the 124 Infy Bde for communication
purposes back to Division.

Runners with messages for Divn will hand
them in at Q Box and thence they will be
transmitted by Motor Cyclist, Telegraph
or usual

(10) The personnel of No 5 Sec will be employed in keeping communication between Machine Gun Companies and their affiliated Brigade H/Q and any further communications that may be required by the O/C Machine Gun Battⁿ.

(11) Acknowledge.

Appendix A duties of Officers attached

23rd Sept 1918.

                 Major.
                 O/C Signals 41 Divⁿ

Copies to 1 41 Div "G"
        2 A.D. Sigs XIX Corps
        3 O.C. Sigs 41st D.S. ⎫
        4   "   "   No 2 Sec ⎬ Appendix "B"
        5   "   "   3 " ⎬ att^d
        6   "   "   4 " ⎭ W/T Instr^{ns}
        7   "   "   5 "
        8 Major Lacey.
        9 Lt Sylvester
       10   " ~~Brennan~~ Stanworth
       11   " ~~Stanworth~~ Brennan
       12 O.C. Signals
       13 Diary
       14 File

SECRET — Duty of Officers.   Appendix "A"

Lt Sylvester.

Lt Sylvester on the afternoon of 24th Sept. you will march with 3 cable wagons to the vicinity of Melon Farm C 26 a or b. You will bivouac there for the night. You will carry with you Rations & Forage for the 25th and 26th Sept.

On the morning of 25 Sept you will move your cable wagons up to the vicinity of Q box and be in position there about 7. a.m. At this point one wagon and detachment under
will come under the orders of O.C. Signals 41 D.A.

You will superintend the laying of the line to the 2nd H/Q of the 124 Infy Bde and will reconnoitre the route to be taken beforehand.

You will await the arrival of 124 Infy Bde at their 2nd H/Q and will then hand over the Cable Wagon to work under orders of O/C No 4 Sec^n Signal Co. and return to Q Box and await further instructions as to the action required with the 3rd Cable Wagon.

Hand barrows and Drums of light Cable will be carried with the Cable Detachments and lines will be laid by hand when the country becomes impassable for Cable Wagons.

Major Lacey you will be responsible that the following lines are working from RR Box on the arrival of Divl. H/Q there.

  a 1 line to the 124 Infy Bde.
  b 1 "   "   123   "
  c 1 "   "   122   "
  d 1 "   "   14th Divn.
  e 1 "   "   35th "
  f 3 "   -   Q Box.

AD Signals XIXth Corps has been asked to provide these lines.

The line to the 122 Infy Bde will be via A.C.2. Box, thence overground.

You will see that the overground portion of the line is laid.

You will be responsible for the working of the Office at RR.

Through the C.Q.M.S. you will be responsible for the supply of Rations and forage.

L̊ Stanworth.

You will be responsible for the Wireless Comm⁽ⁿˢ⁾ and for the supply of Wireless Stores and Accumulators by pack & wheeled transport.

L̊ Brennan.

You will be in charge of the Div¹ Forward Station at Q Box with the assistance of Sgt Cockburn and for establishing and maintaining the Visual Comm⁽ⁿˢ⁾ between Q & RR and any other Visual Communication that may be required later.

You will also assist Lt. Sylvester with his Cable Detachments should he require help.

You will also be in charge of the Div¹ Forward Signal Dump. 1 OR. will assist you in this latter duty.

Any orders as to the movement of the Dump will be issued by O/C. Signals.

Army Form C. 2118.

WAR DIARY
or
INTELLIGENCE SUMMARY.
(Erase heading not required.)

Instructions regarding War Diaries and Intelligence Summaries are contained in F. S. Regs., Part II. and the Staff Manual respectively. Title pages will be prepared in manuscript.

Place	Date	Hour	Summary of Events and Information	Remarks and references to Appendices
Cologne.	10/1/19		Major C. Bellam M.C. R.E. T.C. (from 24th Divisional Signal Coy) assumed command of the company vice Major F.A. Carey M.C.	
			Captain C.H.F. Crawshaw M.C. Off. i/c in Charge Divisional Artillery Signals dismounted.	
			No. 4 I.C. attached 2nd London Bde. relieved No. 3 Sec. attached 2nd London Inf. Bde. at MERHEIM.	
	10/1 - 18/1/19		Nothing to report.	
	19/1/19		Captain J.B. Browning R.E. joined Company from 61st Division Signal Coy. & took over command of Divisional Artillery Signals.	
			Lieut. J.W. Russell M.C. D.C.M. M.M. R.E. T.C. joined Coy. from Reserve Divisional Signal Coy.	
			No. 3 Sec. attd. 2nd London Bde. left HOFNUNGSTHALL & established signal office at ENGELSKIRCHEN. Divisional telegraph & telephone constructed accordingly.	
	20/1/19		Nothing to report.	
	21/1/19		Lieut. C.B. Trenlow (G.L.) joined Coy. from 59th Divisional Signal Coy.	

(Continued)

Army Form C. 2118.

WAR DIARY
or
INTELLIGENCE SUMMARY.
(Erase heading not required.)

Instructions regarding War Diaries and Intelligence Summaries are contained in F. S. Regs., Part II. and the Staff Manual respectively. Title pages will be prepared in manuscript.

Place	Date	Hour	Summary of Events and Information	Remarks and references to Appendices
Cologne.	21/1/19.		Captain J.B.B. Disney M.C. assumed command of the Company vice Major C. Bollam M.C. on leave to U.K.	
	22/1/19.		Lieut. H.L. Stern R.E. joined Coy. from Rhine Army Wireless Section & took over command of Divisional Wireless Section. Lieut. R.J. Senilow R.E.T.C. transferred to Rhine Army School as Officer Instructor. Complete instrs. to make up establishment of Coy. sent rec'd to D.A.D.O.S. + B.S.O. 6th Corps.	
	23/1/19 to 26/1/19		Nothing to report.	
	27/1/19		2/Lts. proceeded to 6th Corps for N.C.O's Course.	
	28/1/19		Lieut. R.S.H. Parker joined Coy. from 149 R.F.A. Bde. & assumed command of 140 Bde. R.F.A. Signal Sub Section.	
	29/1/19 to 3/2/19		Nothing to report.	
	4/2/19		Lieut. J.B. Osborne M.C. Officer in Charge 10.3 Re. attached 2nd London Infantry Bde. demobilised. Lt. B. Gambier (G.L.) assumed command of No. 3 Section attd 2nd London Bde.	

(Continued)

[signature]
Major R?
Comg 6th Corps Signal Coy.

Army Form C. 2118.

WAR DIARY
or
INTELLIGENCE SUMMARY.
(Erase heading not required.)

Instructions regarding War Diaries and Intelligence Summaries are contained in F. S. Regs., Part II. and the Staff Manual respectively. Title pages will be prepared in manuscript.

Place	Date	Hour	Summary of Events and Information	Remarks and references to Appendices
Cologne	5/5/19		85 O.Rs. infantry personnel drawn from the 10th, 11th & 4th Bns. Queens, 9th Bn. East Surreys & 7th Bn. Middlesex attached for instruction with a view to transfer to Signal Service.	
	6/5, 7/5/19		Nothing to report.	
	8/5/19		Lieut. G.P. Slade joined Coy from 6th Corps Signal Coy. for temporary attachment & assumed command of No. 2 Sec. attached 1st London Bde. during the absence of Lieut. C.M. Bell on leave in U.K.	
	9/5 to 10/5/19		Nothing to report.	
			30 O.Rs. infantry personnel drawn from 17th, 23rd & 26th Bns. Royal Fusiliers attached for instruction with a view to transfer to the Signal Service.	
	11/5/19 to 13/5/19		Nothing to report.	
	14/5/19		No. 2 Sec. attached 1st London Bde. relieved No. 4 Sec. attached 3rd London Bde. at MEILENFORST (MERHEIM) No. 4 Sec. attached 3rd London Bde. relieved No. 2 Sec. attached 1st London Bde. at ROSRATH.	

(Continued)

WAR DIARY
or
INTELLIGENCE SUMMARY.
(Erase heading not required.)

Army Form C. 2118.

Place	Date	Hour	Summary of Events and Information	Remarks and references to Appendices
Bologne	15/7/19		Captain J.R Browning Officer in Charge Divisional Artillery Squad appointed Commandant of the Class of Instruction for the training of the attached infantry personnel.	
	16/7/19		Football Match between the boys of the 53rd Bn the Kernchula Fusiliers result - company 5 goals R.E.S 1 goal.	
	17/7/19 & 18/7/19		Nothing to report.	
	19/7/19		36 ORs infantry personnel drawn from 2/4 & 11th Bns Queens & 19th Bn Middlesex attached for instruction with a view to a Signal Service	
	20/7/19 to 30/7/19		Nothing to report.	
	31/7/19		Football Match between boys of the 3rd London and Rifle Boy-lost by 2 goals to 1 Strength of Corps 16 Officers 452 ORs (includes 171 ORs infantry personnel.)	

[signature] Major R.E.
Comdg Corps RE Signals

Army Form C. 2118.

Signals

WAR DIARY
or
INTELLIGENCE SUMMARY.
(Erase heading not required.)

Instructions regarding War Diaries and Intelligence Summaries are contained in F. S. Regs., Part II. and the Staff Manual respectively. Title pages will be prepared in manuscript.

Place	Date	Hour	Summary of Events and Information	Remarks and references to Appendices
Cologne	1/9/19		Church of England Service at 1000 hours Mauberg Barracks. 1 Officer and about 200 other ranks attended.	
	2/9/19		Football Match between Coy and Royal Air Force. Company won by 4 goals to 1.	
	3/9/19		Company Sports held on plot of land adjacent to Mauberg Barracks Parade Ground.	
	4/9/19		Lieut. H.K. Heim R.E. 2/6. Left Company for demobilisation. General Newbegin, Signal Officer in Chief visited Company today. Chief Signals Officer inspected the Classes of Instruction of attached Infantry Personnel.	
	5/9/19		Captain J.B. Bevins awarded Military Cross.	
	6/9/19		Major General Lawford, General Officer Commanding London Division inspected the training and work of the Company. Coy Company 8/0. 65 Marks collected for time to-days favourites.	
	7/9/19		Company paraded at 1000 hours for inspection and afterwards a short Route March. (Continued)	

WAR DIARY
or
INTELLIGENCE SUMMARY.
(Erase heading not required.)

Army Form C. 2118.

Place	Date	Hour	Summary of Events and Information	Remarks and references to Appendices
Cologne	8/9		Usual Church Services at Marienburg Barracks.	
	9/9		In compliance with Commander in Chief's wishes training of infantry personnel continued for the day.	
	14/9		Lecture by Major Rayner Lectch "Non Canvas Association"	
			Cricket Match between Company and 190 Brigade R.F.A. Result:-	
			Company 126 runs, R.F.A. 96 runs	
	15/9		Usual Church Services at Marienburg Barracks.	
	17/9		Company turned out complete with transport for short route march under Captain Dempsey M.C.	
	18/9		3rd London Brigade moved to Unter-Eikenich and Wireless telegraphy detachment.	
			took over Guard Duties at Marienburg Barracks temporarily	
	19/9		No. 1 Section complete with all transport turned out for short route march under 2/Lieut Thurlock.	
			Advance party for further move attached to Engel-Kirchen complete with necessary lines etc to open advanced Divisional	

(Continued)

Army Form C. 2118.

WAR DIARY
or
INTELLIGENCE SUMMARY.
(Erase heading not required.)

Instructions regarding War Diaries and Intelligence Summaries are contained in F. S. Regs., Part II. and the Staff Manual respectively. Title pages will be prepared in manuscript.

Place	Date	Hour	Summary of Events and Information	Remarks and references to Appendices
Cologne	19/9		Headquarters Signal Office. Lieut. Temple Middlesex Regiment attached with a view to transfer to Signal Office.	
	20/9		Paid Company. 2140.50 Marks collected for War Savings Association	
	21/9		Lieut. F.L. Evenard Royal Fusiliers attached to Company with view to transfer to Signal Service.	
	22/9		Usual Church Services at Marienburg Barracks.	
			Football Match between Company and 15th Bn King's Royal Rifles Company won by 2 goals to nil.	
			Captain Richards 2/4th Bn Queens Royal West Surrey Regiment attached to Company.	
	28/9		Cricket Match between Officers and N.C.O.'s of Company and Officers and Men of Women's Royal Air Force. Result W.R.A.F. 110 runs, Company 56 runs.	
	29/9		Usual Church Services at Marienburg Barracks. Samuel party for married personnel – Iraquarters returned to Marienburg.	

(Continued)

Army Form C. 2118.

WAR DIARY
or
INTELLIGENCE SUMMARY.
(Erase heading not required.)

Place	Date	Hour	Summary of Events and Information	Remarks and references to Appendices
Cologne	30/6/19		2nd London Brigade moved from Unter-Bilkerath to Rosrath opening New Signal Office at 1830 hours. Communication established by wireless and lines. Football Match between Company and 18th Bn Kings Royal Rifles. Result Company 1 goal K.R.R's 1 goal.	

Barnett
Major R.E.
Comdg 2nd London Divisional Signal Coy R.E.
3/7/19

WAR DIARY
or
INTELLIGENCE SUMMARY.
(Erase heading not required.)

Army Form C. 2118.

Signal

Instructions regarding War Diaries and Intelligence Summaries are contained in F. S. Regs., Part II. and the Staff Manual respectively. Title pages will be prepared in manuscript.

Place	Date	Hour	Summary of Events and Information	Remarks and references to Appendices
Cologne	1/1/19		Attached Infantry temporarily posted to sections in case of advance, withdrawn and training recommenced.	
"	2/1/19		Cricket Match between 190 Hrs R.F.A. Reserve Company 90 runs R.F.A. 58 runs.	
"	6/1/19		Usual Church Services in Marienburg Barracks.	
"	8/1/19		Cricket Match between Company and 93rd Brigade R.G.A. "D" Battery. Result. "D" Battery 93 runs. Company 37 runs.	
"	9/1/19		Harness Inspection by Major Holmes.	
"	11/1/19		Harness Inspection by Major Holmes M.C.	
"	12/1/19		Cricket Match between Company Royal Air Force and Officers and N.C.O.'s of Company. Result. W.R.A.F. 41 runs. Company 41 runs.	
"	13/1/19		Usual Church Services at Marienburg Barracks.	
"	17/1/19		1st London Brigade moved to Englekirchen. 2nd London Brigade moved to Weilenlorst.	
"	18/1/19		Paid Company 1186 Marks collected for Town Savings Association.	
			(Continued)	

Army Form C. 2118.

WAR DIARY
or
INTELLIGENCE SUMMARY.
(Erase heading not required.)

Place	Date	Hour	Summary of Events and Information	Remarks and references to Appendices
Cologne	19/7/19		In commemoration of the signing of the Peace Treaty a General Holiday for all troops. Authority London Division A/1109 dated 17.7.19.	
"	20/7/19		Muster Church Services at Mauerberg Barracks.	
"	26/7/19		Lieut. R.H. Parks left Company for Demobilization. Forty personnel returned to their respective units.	
"	27/7/19		Muster Church Services at Mauerberg Barracks.	
"	28/7/19		14 Infantry Personnel returned to their respective units. All men released under Army Order 55 have been demobilized. (4 other ranks in Hospital)	

Commanding
London Divisional Signal Company
R.E.

Army Form C. 2118.

WAR DIARY
or
INTELLIGENCE SUMMARY
(Erase heading not required.)

Instructions regarding War Diaries and Intelligence Summaries are contained in F. S. Regs., Part II. and the Staff Manual respectively. Title pages will be prepared in manuscript.

Hour, Date, Place	Summary of Events and Information	Remarks and references to Appendices
1.8.19. Cologne.	The Company £8.12.8 collected for the Savings Association.	
3.8.19. Do.	Usual church services at Mauerburg.	
4.8.19. Do.	General Holiday. Authority :- VI Corps letter No. G.T. 62/3 dated 29.7.19. King's Birthday. Leave granted for Divisional Sports.	
6.8.19. Do.	Usual Church Services at Mauerburg.	
10.8.19. Do.	Capt. G.R.L. Disney M.C. left to take command of the Company vice Major Elphem M.C. who proceeded on leave.	
12.8.19. Do.	Last Company £5.8.7 collected for War Savings Association.	
15.8.19. Do.		

(Continued)

Army Form C. 2118.

WAR DIARY
or
INTELLIGENCE SUMMARY
(Erase heading not required.)

Instructions regarding War Diaries and Intelligence Summaries are contained in F. S. Regs., Part II. and the Staff Manual respectively. Title pages will be prepared in manuscript.

Hour, Date, Place	Summary of Events and Information	Remarks and references to Appendices
17.8.19. Cologne.	Usual Church Services at Marienburg.	
19.8.19. Do.	Company tug-of-war team proceeded to Mehlem to pull against 2nd London Infantry Brigade Trench Mortar Battery for Championship Contest.	
21.8.19. Cologne	Tug of war team turned out for practice field.	
27.8.19. Cologne.	Usual Church Services at Marienburg.	
28.7.19. Do.	Pack Company F.36.1.2. collected for war Service decoration.	
31st 8.19 Do.	Usual Church Services at Marienburg.	
24.8.19. Do.	R.F.A. Personnel attached for lorries borne returned to their respective Brigades.	

[signature]
Major
Officer Commanding
London Divisional Company R.E.

WAR DIARY LONDON DIVISIONAL SIGNAL COMPANY, R.E. Army Form C. 2118.

or

INTELLIGENCE SUMMARY.

(Erase heading not required.)

Instructions regarding War Diaries and Intelligence Summaries are contained in F. S. Regs., Part II. and the Staff Manual respectively. Title pages will be prepared in manuscript.

Place	Date	Hour	Summary of Events and Information	Remarks and references to Appendices
Cologne	9/19 2.		2nd London Infantry Bde moved to Siegburg. Communication advised by wires.	
			Tug of War final with 3rd London I.M.B. Result Company won.	
	7.		Company football in the afternoon, commencing at 1400 hours.	
	8.		Church service held at Mauenburg Barracks and General Church Mauenburg	
	9.		Party of N.C.O.s and men visited Gemünd Lakes	
			Semi-Final 6 Corps Tug of War championship took place at HEUMAR. Company lost.	
	12.		to 93 Bow R.E.I.	
			Company paid £14.14.6 invested in war savings	
	14.		Church service held at Mauenburg Barracks and German Church Mauenburg	
			Cpl/Sgt. Q.[?] was accidentally killed by a German in a car.	
	16.		Divisional horse show held at OVERATH. General Holiday for troops in London Division (Sat.) 1911	
	17.		Funeral of Cpl/Sgt Cyrus W. [?] killed by train took place with full military honours at LINDENTHAL. Firing Party found by 11 Queen's R.O.S. Regt.	
	21.		Church service held at Mauenburg Barracks and German Church Mauenburg	
	26.		Leave to U.K. suspended owing to anticipated Railway Strike in U.K. (early London Div C.1763)	
			Company paid £10.17.0 invested in war savings	

Army Form C. 2118.

WAR DIARY
or
INTELLIGENCE SUMMARY.
(Erase heading not required.)

Instructions regarding War Diaries and Intelligence Summaries are contained in F. S. Regs., Part II. and the Staff Manual respectively. Title pages will be prepared in manuscript.

Place	Date	Hour	Summary of Events and Information	Remarks and references to Appendices
Cologne	9/19 27		Movement of Troops (Demobilization & Leave) suspended until further orders	
			Auth: London Division 9/6 38.	
			[signature] Major R.E.	
			Commanding	
			London Divisional Signal Co R.E.	

www.ingramcontent.com/pod-product-compliance
Lightning Source LLC
Chambersburg PA
CBHW081537160426

43191CB00011B/1778